The
Secret World
of Plants

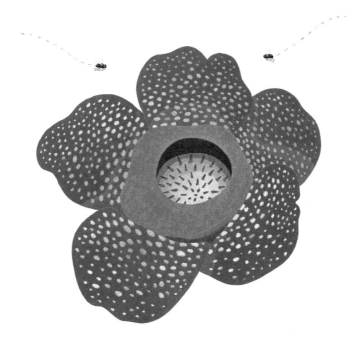

Written by Ben Hoare

Illustrated by Kaley McKean

Contents

LEAVES

STEMS AND TRUNKS

ROOTS AND BULBS

Safety warning

Plants can be interesting to examine and are sometimes very tasty, but be careful—they can also be poisonous to touch or eat. Some people are also allergic to certain plants. If you're not sure what kind of plant you are looking at or if it is safe to handle or eat, always ask an adult for advice. In any case, it's usually a good idea to leave plants alone, to help them thrive, and to allow other people to enjoy the beauty of nature, too.

Introduction

Without plants, life as we know it would not exist.

This book explores the vast plant kingdom. You will meet amazing plants from every continent, learn how they work, and discover the weird and wonderful relationships they have with animals. Plants are extraordinary in so many ways. They may lack eyes or a brain, but they can move, fight, steal, help each other, copy, count, and even learn.

Plants fill the Earth's air with the oxygen we breathe, and they return water to the skies, which produces clouds and rain. They also store carbon, which helps control climate change. Food, fuel, clothes, medicine, and many other things we use every day—plants provide them all.

Today, over a third of the world's plants are under threat. By finding out more about them, we will hopefully do more to care for and protect them. If we do, the planet will be much healthier—for plants and for us.

Ben Hoare
Author

World of plants

Plants are living things that almost always contain a green pigment called chlorophyll. They use this to trap the energy from sunlight and make sugary food. Their roots take in water and other nutrients. So far, we have discovered around 400,000 species of plants, but more are still being found.

Liverworts
Liverworts were some of the first plants on land, appearing around 470 million years ago. They have no leaves, stems, or roots.

Club mosses
These little plants were the first to have stems and veins that carry water. Club mosses appeared about 410 million years ago.

Green algae
These miniature plants live in the sea and freshwater and are the most ancient plants of all. Many have just one cell.

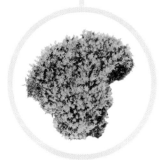

Mosses
About 320 million years old, mosses have simple shoots that are not true leaves, and can only live in damp habitats.

Tree of life
We can use a diagram called a tree of life to show how different plants are related. The first plants to appear on Earth are on branches on the left. Plants that developed more recently are on the right.

Fungi

Fungi may look similar to plants but are a different type of organism. They live in soil and wood or on animals and plants. Most of a fungus is hidden—the part we see, such as a mushroom, is the structure that makes seedlike spores to reproduce.

Lichen

Like fungi, lichens are not plants. Each lichen is a partnership between an alga and a fungus. The alga makes food from sunlight, and the fungus provides water and a body for the partners to share. Lichens are often seen growing on rocks and trees.

Conifers

Conifers lack flowers and produce woody female cones that contain their seeds. Soft male cones make pollen.They appeared around 320 million years ago.

Cycads

Like conifers, cycads have no flowers. The female plants produce seeds in a single huge cone. This group is around 300 million years old.

Flowering plants

Nine-tenths of the world's plants have flowers. When fertilized, the flowers make seeds, which are contained in fruits. This group is more than 130 million years old.

Ferns

Ferns have complex fronds that look like leaves. They first appeared around 360 million years ago and spread with microscopic spores.

Horsetails

Horsetails have tiny leaves, so they use their thick, green stems to harvest energy. Their oldest relatives were about 300 million years old.

7

Leaves

Most plants can make their own food, and their leaves are the factories where it happens. They contain a substance called chlorophyll, which is what makes leaves green. The chlorophyll absorbs light from the Sun to power photosynthesis. This amazing process is how plants make the sugars they need to grow.

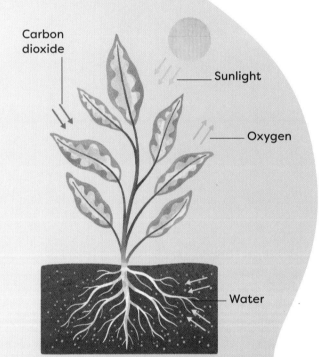

Carbon dioxide

Sunlight

Oxygen

Water

Photosynthesis

Leaves use sunlight to combine carbon dioxide from the air and water from the soil. This chemical reaction produces sugars, which allow the plant to grow. Oxygen is also produced, most of which is released by the leaves.

Deciduous or evergreen?

Deciduous trees drop all their leaves in the fall or the dry season, and replace them in spring or in the rainy season. Their leaves change color before they fall as their chlorophyll breaks down, which reveals other colorful pigments. Evergreen trees have green leaves all year long.

The leaves of evergreen trees stay attached until they become too old. In places with lots of sunshine and rain, this allows trees to photosynthesize year round.

Dropping their foliage lets deciduous trees both save energy and get rid of waste products that have built up in their leaves.

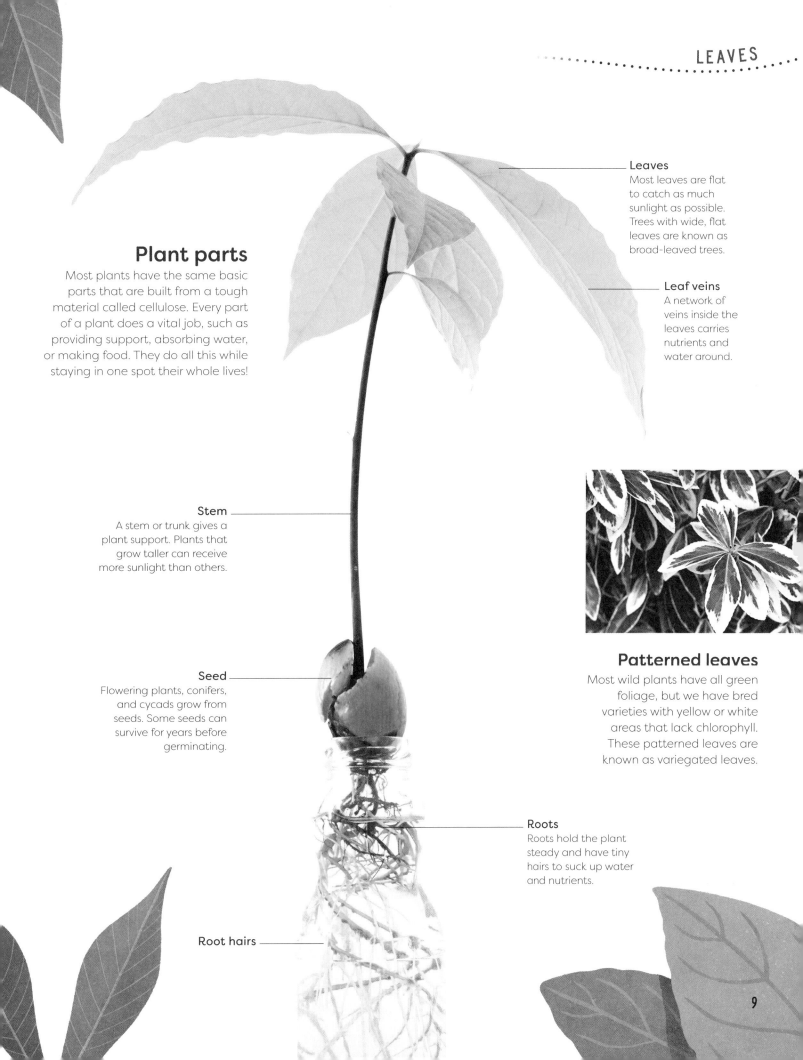

Plant parts

Most plants have the same basic parts that are built from a tough material called cellulose. Every part of a plant does a vital job, such as providing support, absorbing water, or making food. They do all this while staying in one spot their whole lives!

Leaves
Most leaves are flat to catch as much sunlight as possible. Trees with wide, flat leaves are known as broad-leaved trees.

Leaf veins
A network of veins inside the leaves carries nutrients and water around.

Stem
A stem or trunk gives a plant support. Plants that grow taller can receive more sunlight than others.

Seed
Flowering plants, conifers, and cycads grow from seeds. Some seeds can survive for years before germinating.

Patterned leaves

Most wild plants have all green foliage, but we have bred varieties with yellow or white areas that lack chlorophyll. These patterned leaves are known as variegated leaves.

Roots
Roots hold the plant steady and have tiny hairs to suck up water and nutrients.

Root hairs

Flowers

Most plants reproduce with flowers, which are often colorful and give off a powerful scent. However, they are not for our benefit. Their job is to attract insects, birds, or mammals, which will carry pollen from one flower to another. In return, flowers usually reward these animals with a sweet liquid, called nectar.

Parts of a flower

A flower's petals are advertisements announcing free food to pollinators. They come in many shapes and sizes. The male and female parts of the flower are in the middle of the petals, and these are what will produce the plant's seeds.

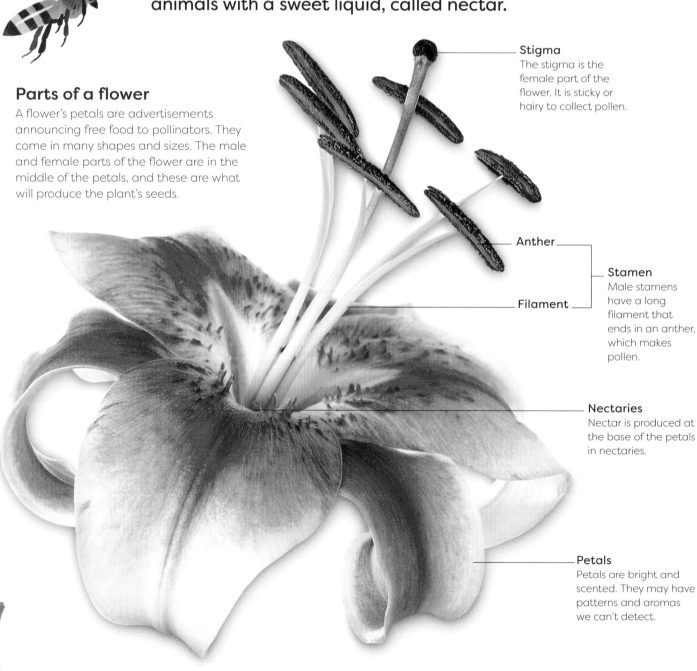

Stigma
The stigma is the female part of the flower. It is sticky or hairy to collect pollen.

Anther

Filament

Stamen
Male stamens have a long filament that ends in an anther, which makes pollen.

Nectaries
Nectar is produced at the base of the petals in nectaries.

Petals
Petals are bright and scented. They may have patterns and aromas we can't detect.

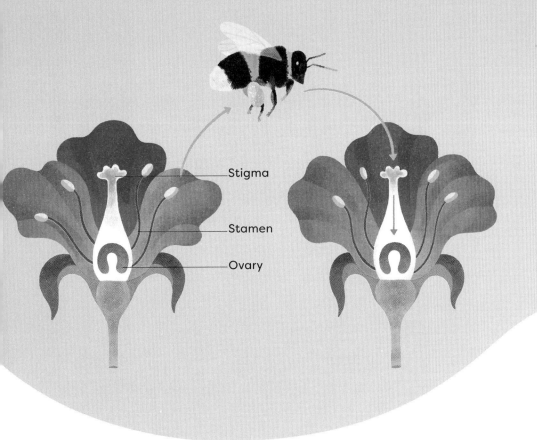

Stigma

Stamen

Ovary

Pollination

Pollination occurs when pollen is moved from the stamen of one flower to the stigma of another flower of the same type, usually by a pollinator or the wind. The pollen then grows a tube that takes the male pollen cells to the ovary. There, they join with female cells in a process called fertilization. The fertilized ovary makes seeds.

Fruits and seeds

When a flower has been fertilized, its ovary swells up and becomes a fruit. The fruit can contain one seed or many. Figs are made from lots of small fruits—each with one seed— that have joined up.

Female
squash flower

Male
squash flower

Male and female flowers

Some plants have separate male and female flowers, which can be produced either on separate plants or different parts of the same plant. The male flowers have only stamens, while the female flowers have stigmas.

11

Seeds

A seed is one of the neatest packages in the natural world. Inside, there is everything that a baby plant, called an embryo, needs to start growing. The embryo rests until it senses the right moment has come to sprout. It may be waiting weeks, months, or even years!

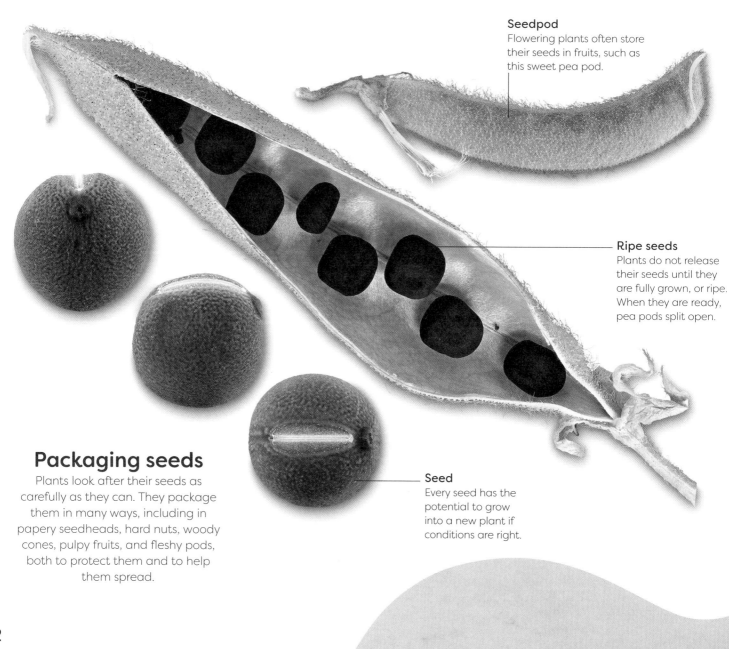

Seedpod
Flowering plants often store their seeds in fruits, such as this sweet pea pod.

Ripe seeds
Plants do not release their seeds until they are fully grown, or ripe. When they are ready, pea pods split open.

Seed
Every seed has the potential to grow into a new plant if conditions are right.

Packaging seeds
Plants look after their seeds as carefully as they can. They package them in many ways, including in papery seedheads, hard nuts, woody cones, pulpy fruits, and fleshy pods, both to protect them and to help them spread.

Inside a seed

Most seeds have a tough coat. This protects the embryo and its waiting root and shoot. There is also a food supply, which is in a pair of seed leaves or stored separately.

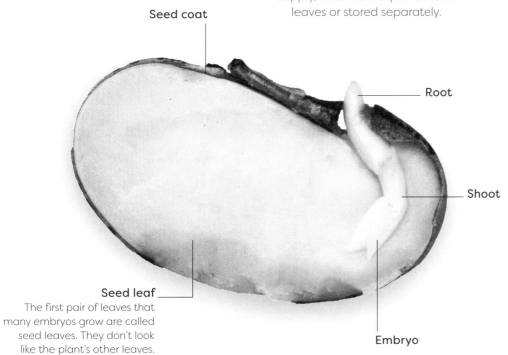

Seed coat

Root

Shoot

Embryo

Seed leaf
The first pair of leaves that many embryos grow are called seed leaves. They don't look like the plant's other leaves.

Seed banks

People preserve seeds in seed banks. They can be used to grow new plants in the future, and protect species frrom going extinct.

Germination

A seed will usually only sprout, or germinate, when it's in the dark. It must also have water, oxygen, and be at a suitable temperature. When conditions are perfect, it begins to absorb water and its root and shoot emerge. The new plant is called a seedling.

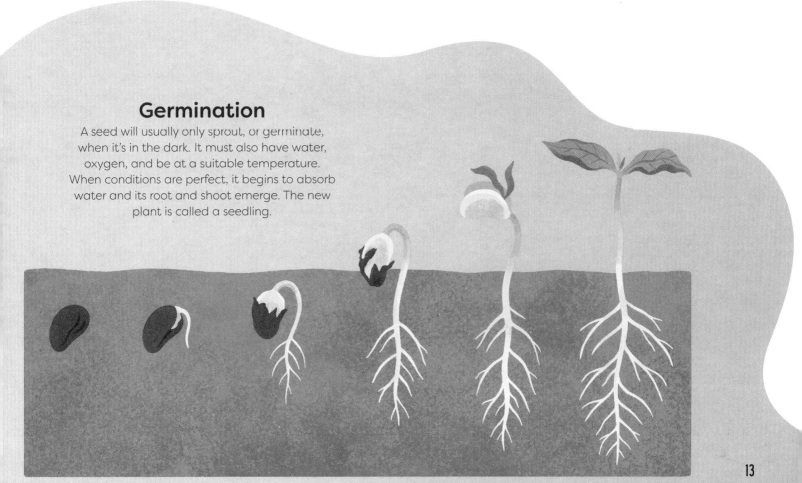

13

CHAPTER 1

Leaves

Leaves make Earth green, and they are vital organs to most plants. During the day, they absorb energy from sunlight, like solar panels. They are also lungs, through which plants breathe. Many leaves are flat, but they come in all sorts of other shapes, such as sharp spines, needles, and toothed blades. The simplest and most ancient plants lack leaves but they have other parts that function in a similar way.

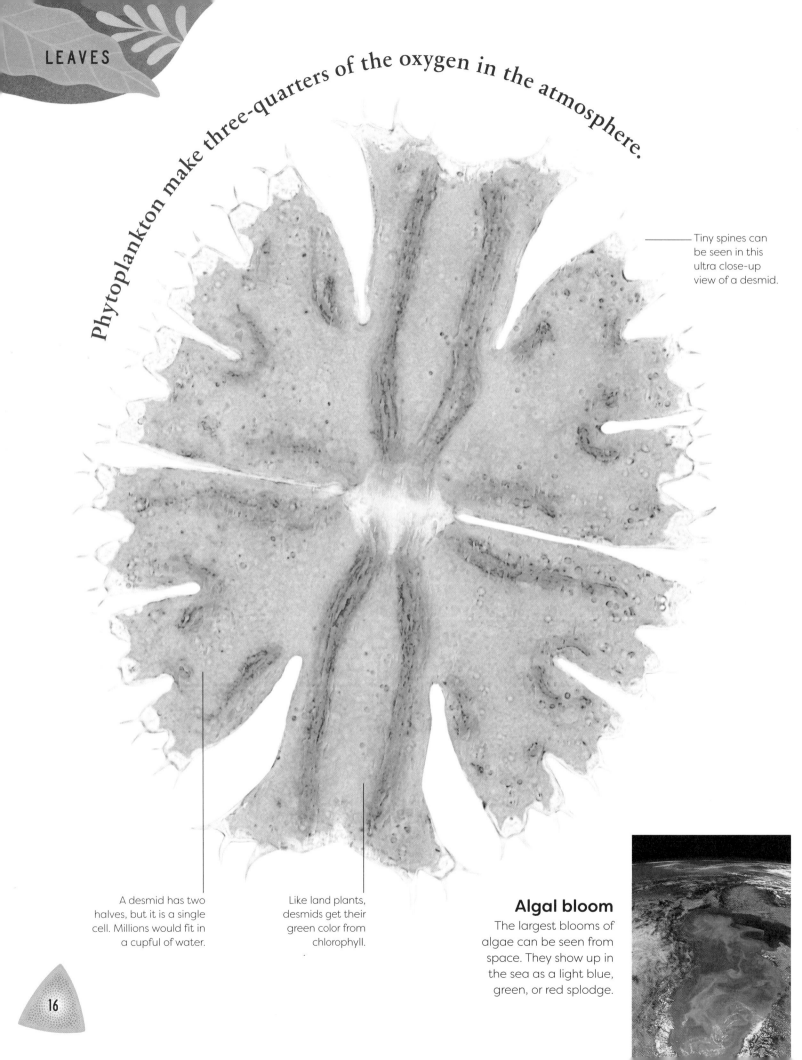

Phytoplankton make three-quarters of the oxygen in the atmosphere.

Tiny spines can be seen in this ultra close-up view of a desmid.

A desmid has two halves, but it is a single cell. Millions would fit in a cupful of water.

Like land plants, desmids get their green color from chlorophyll.

Algal bloom

The largest blooms of algae can be seen from space. They show up in the sea as a light blue, green, or red splodge.

Phytoplankton

These micro-plants live in water and make most of the oxygen we breathe.

Earth's most important plants are also the tiniest. They are phytoplankton. Their name comes from the Ancient Greek words phyto, which means "plant," and plankton, meaning "to drift". Billions upon billions of them float through the planet's oceans and freshwater. There are many different types, including diatoms, cyanobacteria, and green algae, with thousands of species each. Most of them have only one cell and are no wider than a human hair. These microscopic life forms lack leaves but many count as plants because they contain something that almost every plant has—chlorophyll. Just like other plants, they use it to harvest sunlight, which they turn into sugar through photosynthesis. Cyanobacteria were the first organisms to carry out this process, around 2.7 billion years ago.

Phytoplankton live near the water's surface because that is where they can capture the most sunlight. Often they multiply in vast swarms known as blooms. Some ocean blooms are as large as cities! There are so many phytoplankton on Earth, all carrying out photosynthesis, that they release more oxygen than all of the world's land plants put together.

Desmid
(*Micrasterias apiculata*)
Bright green desmids are a type of green alga found in freshwater. They are one of many very different types of phytoplankton, including cyanobacteria and diatoms.

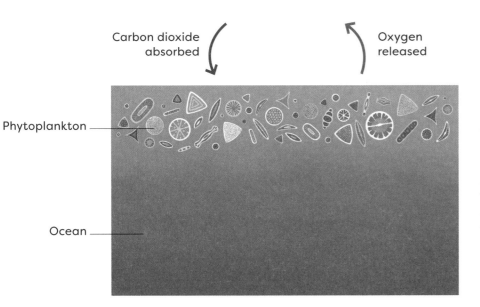

Carbon dioxide absorbed

Oxygen released

Phytoplankton

Ocean

Ocean oxygen
Life in the ocean depends on phytoplankton, which take in carbon dioxide and give off oxygen. The oxygen is used by all sorts of animals, including air-breathing whales. In turn, whale poo contains nitrogen and iron, which help the phytoplankton grow.

Sphagnum moss

This ancient bog plant can soak up huge amounts of water like a sponge.

Soft, green mosses have the simplest kind of leaves. They don't have roots or strong stems, so they hug the ground rather than grow upward. Yet the uncomplicated structure of mosses has been a great success. There have been mosses on Earth for hundreds of millions of years, and they have survived periods of enormous change. Sphagnum moss lives in peat bogs and moorland, where it rains a lot. It spreads over the wet ground for miles in every direction. If you squelch across it, you will discover it is like damp fur or a soggy carpet. The moss is so absorbent, it can hold 20 times its own weight in water. Sometimes, it grows on the surface of pools to form a floating mat, so watch your step!

Peat bog water is acidic. This means sphagnum moss is too, which gives it an amazing ability to kill harmful bacteria. In the past, people dried out sphagnum moss to wrap up wounds, helping them heal. Great quantities of the moss were gathered during World War I to provide dressings in hospitals.

Sphagnum moss
(Sphagnum)
There are hundreds of types of this moss, which cover vast areas in cool, wet parts of the world. They are among the main plants in the Arctic.

Making peat
Over thousands of years, dead sphagnum moss slowly piles up. The plant material underneath is squashed down and eventually it turns into a rich soil called peat. Just 0.04 in (1 mm) of peat forms each year. Peat is dug up to grow plants in, but because it stores so much carbon, it is best left in bogs!

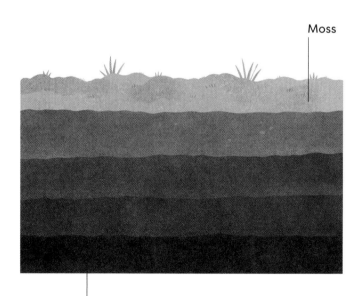

Moss

Peat

Dried sphagnum moss was once used instead of diapers!

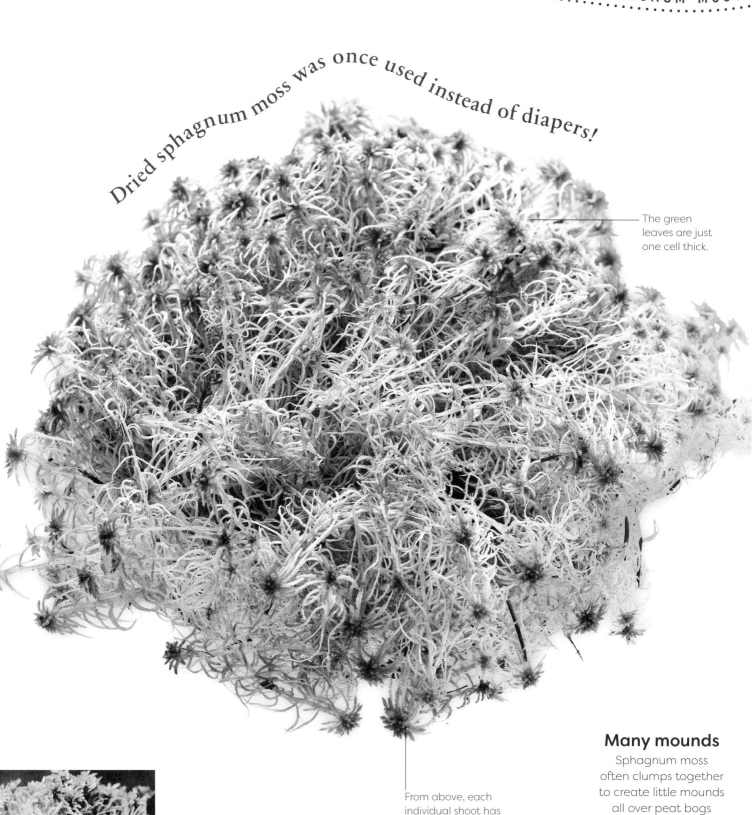

The green leaves are just one cell thick.

From above, each individual shoot has a star shape.

Many mounds

Sphagnum moss often clumps together to create little mounds all over peat bogs and moors.

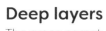

Deep layers

The green carpet of living moss grows on top of a thick yellow and brown layer of dead moss. The dead moss layer in bogs may be 33 ft (10 m) deep.

19

Ancient plants

The first land plants appeared around 500 million years ago. They developed into a wonderful variety of species, including mosses and liverworts that crept across the ground, and treelike giants that formed the first forests. Some tough ancient plants survive to this day.

Ginkgo

Forests of ginkgo trees once covered much of the world, but this Chinese species is the only member of its ancient family left. It has beautiful fan-shaped leaves.

Deer fern

Ferns live in wet, shady forests and have feathery leaves, known as fronds. They spread by releasing millions of dustlike particles called spores from their fronds.

Tamarisk moss

This moss has fluffy shoots, which are not true leaves. Like other mosses around the world, it lives in damp places and grows very slowly near to the ground.

Sprenger's magnolia

Magnolia trees date from the time of the dinosaurs. Their big, tough flowers are pollinated by beetles because these trees appeared before many other insects existed.

Dawn redwood

This coniferous tree was once common in cold, northern lands. It was believed to be extinct until it was rediscovered in the 1940s in China.

Wollemi pine

Until 1994, we only knew these tall conifers from fossils. Then a small group was found in an Australian rain forest. Today, the location of the wild trees is kept a secret.

Nonvascular
moss

Vascular fern

Two kinds of plants

The most ancient plants alive are small and simple, such as mosses and liverworts. They are called nonvascular plants. The rest, including ferns and flowering plants, are known as vascular plants because they have veins to transport water, food, and minerals—like blood flowing through our bodies.

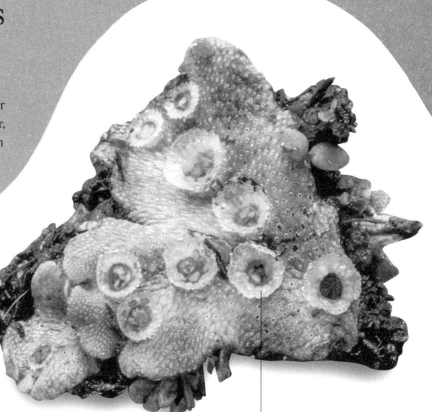

Common liverwort

Liverworts are one of the oldest plants of all and often look like slimy scraps of lettuce. They lack roots, stems, and leaves, so they take in water directly through their surface.

These cuplike structures are nurseries for baby liverworts.

Mediterranean clubmoss

Clubmosses have veins to carry water, so they are able to grow taller than liverworts and mosses—which are not related to them. Some have small, upright stems like miniature fir trees.

The stems are covered in flat leaves that look like teeth.

All parts of cycads are highly poisonous.

Spiral leaves
The cycad's leaves all sprout from its base and grow in a tight spiral around the trunk.

Sago palm leaves can grow up to 5 ft (1.5 m) long and remain green all year.

Toxic seeds
Clusters of bright red seeds develop in fertilized female cones. They are the most poisonous part of the plant.

A whole new cycad can grow from the main plant's trunk.

Cycad

Cycads were some of the first plants to attract insects, using cones instead of flowers.

If we could go on a prehistoric plant safari, we would see many cycads. Some would be the size of bushes, while others would tower over our heads like trees. We know from studying fossils that these magnificent plants have been on Earth for more than 300 million years. Most died out long ago, but some species of cycads still flourish in warm parts of the world. One of the best-known of these ancient survivors is the sago palm. Its name is confusing, because it is not a palm, though its long leaves do look like those of palm trees.

Every cycad is either male or female. The male plants draw in beetles to take their pollen to female plants. However, cycads don't have flowers. The males' pollen is produced inside a tough, woody structure called a cone. Female cycads also have a cone to receive the pollen. Female cones are much larger. In sago palms, they are the size of basketballs, but in other cycads they can be as big as barrels and weigh the same as a six-year-old child!

Sago palm
(Cycas revoluta)
This cycad originally comes from islands in southern Japan, where the climate is warm and wet. It is now grown around the world.

Male cone

Female cone

Beetle pollinators

Male cycads produce a single hard cone that contains pollen. Pollen-eating beetles are attracted to it. If the beetles then visit a female cycad, some of the sticky pollen rubs off onto the huge female cone. The fertilized cone now develops seeds.

Branching leaflets
A fern frond has smaller leaflets that branch off to the left and right. They are equally spaced to form two parallel columns.

The first tree ferns lived long before the dinosaurs.

Spore factories
Underneath the frond, there are many neat rows of little brown lumps, called sori. They produce the fern's spores.

Each leaflet is divided into many smaller sections.

Tree fern

These ferns have turned into giants, with feathery fronds that rise above the forest floor.

Many plants can't survive in deep shade, but you will find ferns in the darkest parts of a forest, often under trees. The damp, cool conditions here suit them perfectly. Most ferns would not come any higher than your waist; however, even shade-loving ferns need some sunlight, and tree ferns steal as much as they can by growing taller than other plants. Some are enormous—the largest species can reach 66 ft (20 m) high. They live in rain-drenched forests in Australia, New Zealand, Hawaii, and other Pacific islands.

If you touch a tree fern's trunk, you can tell it isn't a real tree because its wrinkled surface is not woody—it is actually a mat of old roots. Another difference is in the leaves, known as fronds, which have a beautiful shape like a bird's feather. Many ferns have fronds like this, with a repeating pattern that increases their surface area to capture as much daylight as possible. Ferns don't have flowers, and don't make pollen and seeds. They reproduce by releasing tens of millions of spores—specks of material too small to see that are released into the air on dry days.

New Zealand tree fern
(Dicksonia squarrosa)
New Zealand's wettest forests are home to this tree fern. It grows as tall as a giraffe.

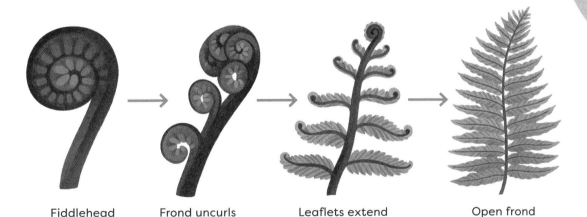

Fiddlehead → Frond uncurls → Leaflets extend → Open frond

Birth of a frond
A new fern frond, called a fiddlehead, is curled up tight like a roll of paper. The frond uncurls while it pushes upward. As it continues to grow, many symmetrical leaflets extend on each side of the stem.

Colossal leaves

Plants compete with each other for sunlight, so it helps
to have large, fast-growing leaves. The prickly leaves of
giant rhubarb—which is not related to the rhubarb
found in stores—are wider than a double bed! They are
able to capture lots of light, while the slower-growing
plants underneath them are left in the shade.

Spiral pattern

When viewed from above, the leaves can be seen to spiral around their branch. This pattern enables as many leaves as possible to be packed together.

The monkey puzzle tree is the national tree of Chile.

The leaves have a glossy surface and viciously sharp tip.

The entire branch is completely covered in leaves.

Long-life leaves

Monkey puzzle leaves stay green and healthy for an incredibly long time. Some stay on the tree for more than 15 years, much longer than the leaves on most other trees.

Monkey puzzle tree

Tough leaves give this tree heavy-duty armor against browsing animals.

Some trees make a huge effort not to be eaten, and none more so than the monkey puzzle tree. Its leaves are so sharp, they can draw blood. They are also extremely thick and packed together like a reptile's overlapping scales. This species was alive during the Jurassic Period, around 150 million years ago, when there were long-necked dinosaurs whose diet was made up of tree leaves, so the tree needed serious protection. Some scientists think that the monkey puzzle tree's impressive height may also be a defense. Perhaps the tree is trying to put its leaves out of reach.

It is said that the monkey puzzle tree was given its curious name because it is so spiky, it would puzzle a monkey trying to climb it. In fact, the tree's huge seeds are eaten by squirrels, not monkeys! The Mapuche people of South America also harvest the seeds, and roast them like chestnuts. When monkey puzzle trees die, their wood can become squashed down over millions of years to form jet, a black gemstone.

Monkey puzzle tree
(Araucaria araucana)

The Andes Mountains in Argentina and Chile are the original home of this tree, but it has been planted in parks and gardens worldwide.

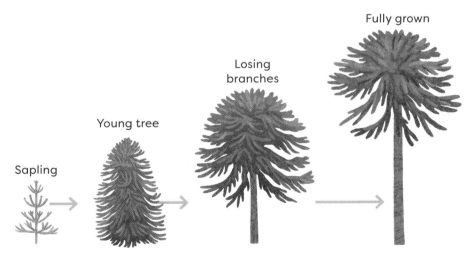

Fully grown

Losing branches

Young tree

Sapling

Changing shape

A monkey puzzle tree begins growing like most other saplings. However, as it gets older, the lower branches drop off. After hundreds of years, the mature tree has a tall, straight trunk with all of its branches at the top.

Aspen leaves and bark are food for deer and moose.

Deciduous leaves drop off in the fall after they have changed color.

Each leaf has a rounded, heartlike shape.

Old bark

The bark of the quaking aspen is whitish and beautifully smooth. In older trees, it becomes darker and wrinkled near the ground.

Color change

In fall, the green chlorophyll in quaking aspen leaves starts to break down. Then the leaves' yellow and orange pigments become visible.

The stalk is flat and extremely long.

Quaking aspen

Aspen leaves rustle in the breeze, and in fall turn a spectacular gold color.

You can identify the quaking aspen with your eyes closed, just from the sound it makes. Its leaves tremble in even a gentle wind, so the entire tree seems to be on the move, and the soothing chorus is like running water or people whispering. The constant fluttering is caused by the tree's unusual leaf stalks, which are flat and catch any air currents. It is a mystery why they do this. One theory is that it enables sunlight to reach every part of the leaves, including those lower down the tree.

Quaking aspens usually spread from their roots. Within a few years, a parent tree is standing in the middle of many saplings. The parent shares carbon and other nutrients through the roots, as if caring for its young. One aspen colony in the state of Utah has 45,000 trees! The colony weighs probably 6,600 tons (6,000 tonnes) and could be 80,000 years old. All of the trees are connected and have identical genes, which means they are a single massive living thing.

Quaking aspen
(Populus tremuloides)
The quaking aspen is found in cool regions of North America, often in mountains, from the Arctic to Mexico.

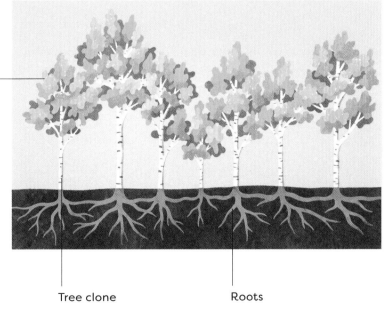

Clones change color together

Tree clone

Roots

Root system
Young aspen trees shoot up from roots belonging to the parent tree, and share the same root network. The new trees, called clones, are exact copies of the parent. In fall, their leaves all change color and drop at the same time.

Venus flytrap

This little plant has deadly leaves that catch insects and other prey.

Some plants are killers. The Venus flytrap is one of them, yet it grows just a couple of inches tall and has leaves no bigger than an adult human's thumbnail. Its special trick is that its leaves can snap shut. If a beetle, ant, spider, or fly crawls over a leaf, it closes like a pair of jaws with incredible speed, then digests the prey using acid similar to our own stomach juices. However, the Venus flytrap doesn't catch prey for food, because its green leaves can make sugar by photosynthesis, like other plants. Why, then, is it so deadly? The answer is that it kills for minerals. The soil it lives in lacks nitrogen and phosphorus, so it obtains these from animals.

So that the Venus flytrap knows if a bit of dead leaf or twig has landed on it rather than a real animal, it has trigger hairs inside its leaves that can count! If a hair is touched more than once in a short space of time, the leaf reacts to the movement by snapping the trap shut on the prey.

Venus flytrap
(Dionaea muscipula)
This carnivorous plant lives in wetlands on the east coast of the US. It is rare in the wild, but it is grown in large numbers to be sold as a house plant.

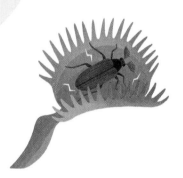

1) An insect arrives
A flytrap leaf is red and shiny inside and produces nectar. The bright color and sweet treat attract insects.

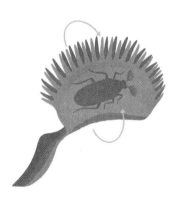

2) The trap shuts
The leaf waits for an insect to touch a trigger hair twice, or touch two hairs, within 20 seconds. Then it snaps shut.

3) Digestion begins
As the insect touches more hairs, the closed leaf fills with digestive juices to dissolve it. A week or so later, it opens again.

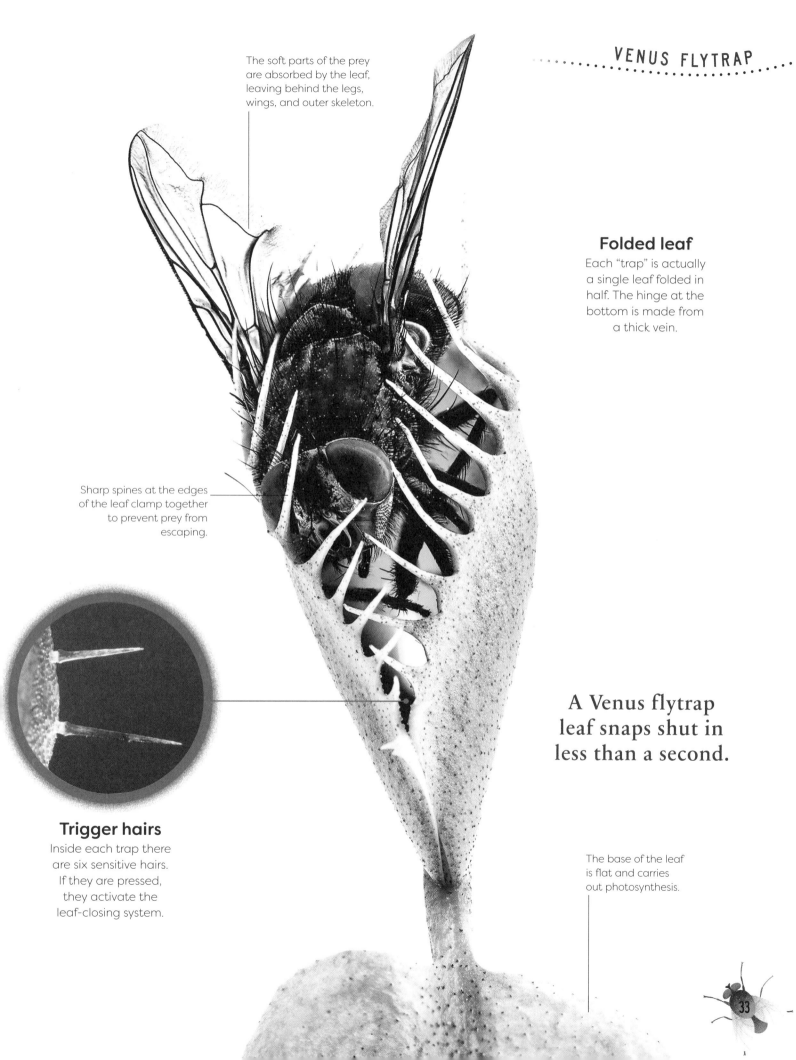

The soft parts of the prey are absorbed by the leaf, leaving behind the legs, wings, and outer skeleton.

Folded leaf

Each "trap" is actually a single leaf folded in half. The hinge at the bottom is made from a thick vein.

Sharp spines at the edges of the leaf clamp together to prevent prey from escaping.

A Venus flytrap leaf snaps shut in less than a second.

Trigger hairs

Inside each trap there are six sensitive hairs. If they are pressed, they activate the leaf-closing system.

The base of the leaf is flat and carries out photosynthesis.

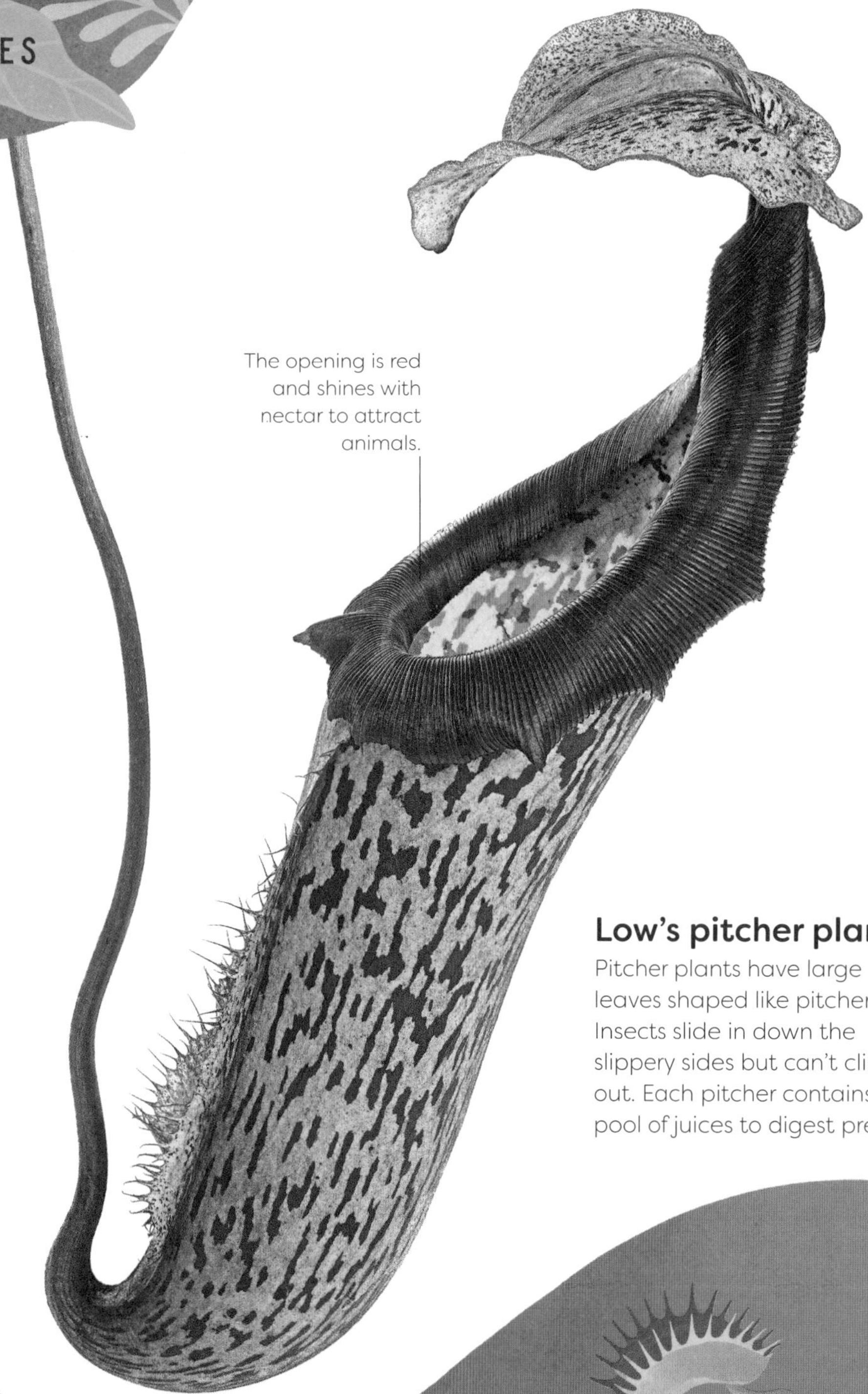

The tall, pitcherlike leaves can reach 3 ft (1 m) high.

The opening is red and shines with nectar to attract animals.

White trumpet pitcher

Each leaf of a trumpet pitcher is shaped into a long tube. When insects investigate the nectar at the top, they fall in, and hairs on the inside of the tube stop them from escaping.

Low's pitcher plant

Pitcher plants have large leaves shaped like pitchers. Insects slide in down the slippery sides but can't climb out. Each pitcher contains a pool of juices to digest prey.

Snap trap

Suction trap

Types of trap

Some plants have active traps that snap shut on insects or suck them in. Others wait for victims to stick to their leaves and stems, or drop into pitfall traps. A few have underground leaves that catch worms.

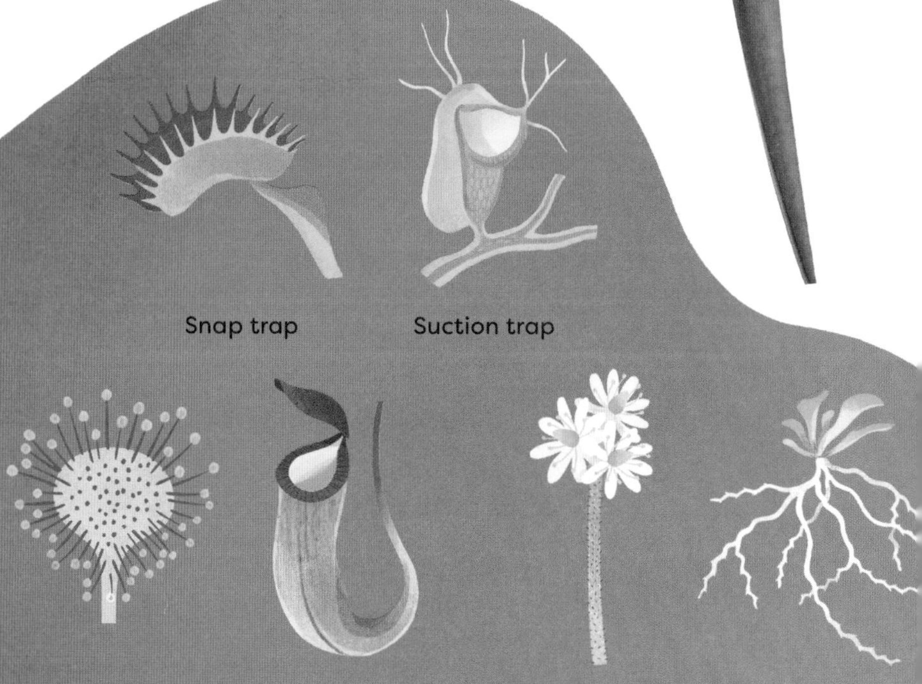

Sticky leaves

Pitfall trap

Sticky stem

Underground leaves

Meat-eating plants

Over 700 species of plants catch and kill animals. Most live in marshy places or wet tropical forests, where the boggy soil lacks nutrients. They obtain the minerals they need from their victims instead. These plants are often called insectivorous, because insects are their main prey.

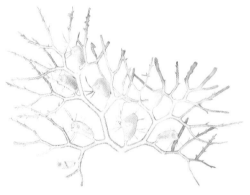

Greater bladderwort

This pond plant has underwater leaves like tiny, see-through balloons. The "balloons" have trigger hairs, and if an insect touches one, it is sucked inside with lightning speed.

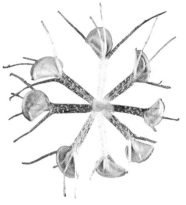

Waterwheel plant

The leaves of this aquatic plant are arranged like the spokes of a wheel. They have hinged traps, which slam shut if they feel a water flea swim past.

Butterwort

Butterwort leaves look shiny, which attracts flies, but the tempting surface is actually deadly slime. As soon as the insects land, they become stuck and are digested.

Cobra plant

This snakelike plant might remind you of a cobra. Insects enter the "head" in search of nectar, then find there's no exit. The plant uses bacteria to break them down.

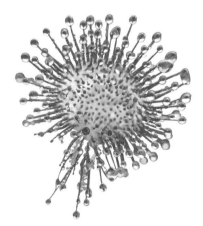

Round-leaved sundew

Sundews are covered in red hairs, and each one ends in what seems to be a droplet of nectar. This is glue, though! The leaves fold up to digest insects that become stuck.

Mother of thousands

This curious plant grows dozens of babies on its frilly leaves.

The mother of thousands can spread without seeds, and the way it does so is beautifully simple. It produces many tiny replicas of itself. There are not thousands of them—the plant's name is an exaggeration—but each plant can grow more than a hundred. All of the new plantlets have exactly the same genetic makeup as the mother of thousands that produces them. They therefore grow up to become perfect copies, or clones. One day, these copies will also produce plantlets, and these will be clones too.

Each of the plantlets, or pups, starts life as a minuscule bud on the side of a leaf. This quickly develops its own circular leaf a fraction of an inch long and grows roots. Eventually, it falls from the parent and continues its development in the ground. Spreading this way has advantages. As the pups already have roots and leaves when they detach, they have a head start, compared to a seed. It is also a fast way to reproduce, since it doesn't require flowers that need to be pollinated, so the mother of thousands can cover large areas rapidly.

Mother of thousands
(Kalanchoe daigremontiana)
This type of Kalanchoe comes from the island of Madagascar, off the east coast of Africa. Although poisonous, it is a popular house plant because it can survive with little water.

Storing water
The mother of thousands stores masses of water in its thick leaves, so it can survive months with little or no rain.

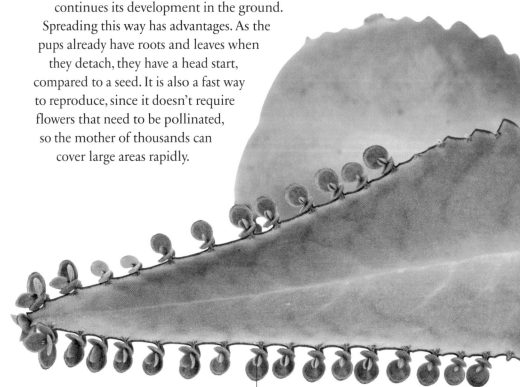

The plantlets are spaced evenly along the leaf's edge.

Pups on leaf

Parent plant

Plant factory

It takes two or three years for mother of thousands to reach full size and produce baby plants. The pups drop off and take root in the ground, scattered around their parent. When they grow up, they repeat the cycle.

New plants

Root growth

The pups start to form their own roots while still attached to the parent. Until they fall off, the pups get nutrients from the parent leaf.

37

The leaflets roll up into bundles, which lie against the leaf stem.

Fluffy flower heads

The plant's pink flower heads look like fluffy pom-poms or exploding fireworks. Each flower head is made up of many tiny flowers.

This species is also called the touch-me-not plant.

Divided leaf

Every leaf has two neat rows of leaflets, which are joined to the stem in pairs. Each pair of leaflets shuts at the same moment.

Sensitive plant

If anything touches the sensitive plant, it senses danger and closes its leaves.

A hungry caterpillar that crawls onto the sensitive plant is in for a shock. Within a few seconds, its leaves close up and start to droop. What was a juicy meal has turned into a bundle of rolled-up stems covered in prickles. The plant appears to have died! So the caterpillar moves on to find something easier to eat. With the threat over, the sensitive plant is able to relax and open its leaves again.

This amazing plant has fascinated many scientists, including Charles Darwin in the 19th century. Even gently blowing on it makes it instantly react. How can it move its leaves in such an animal-like way? Some people decided it must be half-plant and half-animal, but today we know the truth. Like all plants, the sensitive plant lacks muscles and nerves. However, its leaves are divided into pairs of oval leaflets, and when it is touched, the plant sends an electrical pulse to the leaflets. The signal instructs the leaflets to release water. The pressure inside the leaflets suddenly drops, making them collapse and fold.

Sensitive plant
(*Mimosa pudica*)
Central and South America are the original home of this plant, but it grows as a weed all over the tropics. It is a member of the pea family, but it isn't edible.

| Leaves open | | Leaves begin to close | | Leaves fully closed |

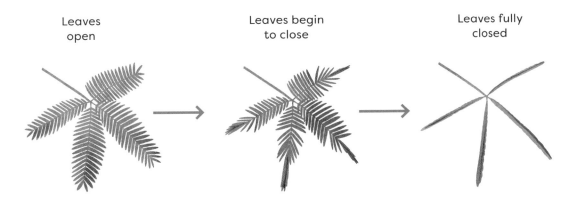

Closing leaves

When the sensitive plant closes its leaves, the action moves rapidly along each stem. First one leaflet closes, then its neighbor follows, and the one after that, until the entire leaf is shut. It looks like a line of dominoes toppling over.

Plants that move

Plants are rooted to the spot, but they can still move. They shift position by twisting their stems and by turning or closing their leaves and flowers. This enables them to capture the most daylight, to rest at night, and even to avoid being eaten.

Common sunflower

The buds of these common flowers start every day facing the sunrise in the east. They twist to track the Sun as it moves across the sky, and end the day pointing west.

Dancing plant

The leaves of this plant have an extra little leaflet on their stem, which can move up and down as if dancing. This might put off insects from eating the plant.

Common daisy

Daisies open their flowers in the day, when their pollinators are active. At night, when these insects stop visiting, the flowers close to protect their pollen and keep it dry.

Birdcage evening primrose

When this plant dies, it dries up and its stems curl into a ball. The entire plant can then roll away in the wind, spreading its seeds as it bounces over the ground.

Tamarind

Every evening, the feathery leaves of the tamarind tree fold up neatly. Scientists think it may be to keep the leaves from losing water overnight while the tree is resting.

Trigger plant

A trigger plant has a long "club" on its flower, and as soon as a bee lands, it reacts fast. The club springs up to slap pollen onto the back of the bee.

Prayer plant

The prayer plant is named for the way its leaves fold up at night, probably to save water. The folded leaves can look like the hands of someone praying.

A bump in the leaf's stem is where it moves from.

A fern frond has hundreds of tiny spore launchers grouped within spots.

Common polypody

Some ferns, such as this one, use a powerful launch system to scatter the microscopic spores gathered on the underside of their leaves. When it fires, it flings the spores through the air with tremendous force.

Plant body clocks

All plants, like animals, have a kind of internal clock. This allows them to do things at the right time of day or night. For example, they might open or close their flowers and leaves, and start or stop photosynthesis.

Nighttime

Daytime

41

European larch

With thin needles for leaves, larch trees can survive extreme cold for months on end.

An immense forest circles the Arctic, stretching like a vast belt around Alaska, Canada, Scandinavia, and Siberia. This is the boreal forest and it may have as many as 750 billion trees! A great number of them are larches, which are a beautiful type of conifer. These tough trees are also found high up in chilly mountain ranges. Larches, like many conifers—including pines, firs, and spruces—have needlelike leaves with a waxy surface. Freshwater is in short supply in the freezing forest because it is locked up in ice or snow. Needles help these trees cope with the dry conditions because they lose very little water. Conifers growing in hot, dry areas benefit from the same water-saving leaves.

Most conifers are evergreen, keeping their needles all year, but larches are different. In fall, their needles turn golden, then fall off as winter approaches, leaving just the trees' woody cones attached to their branches. Larches also produce a natural antifreeze, which fills their wood and bark to prevent ice damage. It is made from a super-strong cocktail of proteins, starches, and sugars.

European larch
(*Larix decidua*)
Forests with these trees are common in Europe's mountains, and they are widely planted for their useful wood.

Through the seasons
All summer, the European larch has green needles like any other conifer. However, in fall, it turns a dazzling golden yellow, so the tree stands out against its always-green relatives. The needles drop in winter, and regrow in spring.

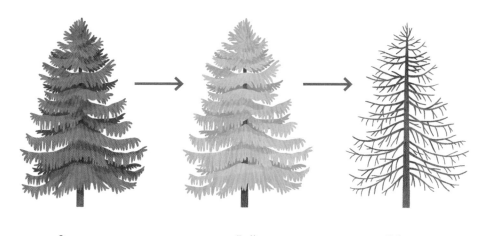

Summer   Fall   Winter

Spring cones

Larch trees have separate male and female cones. The young pink female cones are called "larch roses." These develop into hard cones full of seeds.

Pointed needles

Larch needles contain green chlorophyll. However, because their surface area is small, they are less effective at photosynthesis than flat leaves.

Larch branches slope down, so that heavy snow slides off.

The needles are thin and up to 2 in (4 cm) long.

Tufts of needles sprout from twigs.

43

Many shades

The natural color of bougainvillea is a deep shade of pink, but plant breeders have created red, white, and yellow varieties.

Bougainvillea bracts are as bright as lipstick!

Three flowers are grouped within each collar of bracts, and attract bees, which pollinate them.

Bright bracts

The flamingo flower has scarlet, heart-shaped bracts. The yellow spike in the center consists of many tiny flowers.

The bracts are as thin as tissue paper and partially see-through.

44

Bougainvillea

Many of the leaves on this plant are so colorful, they look more like petals.

Sometimes, leaves are not what they seem. You might think this climbing plant from tropical South America is covered in masses of pink blossom. Yet the spectacular display is produced not by petals, but by a special type of leaf called a bract. Many plants have bracts, which protect the developing buds or flowers. They are usually green like the rest of the leaves, so you may not notice them. A few plants, however, have large, colorful bracts. Those of bougainvillea are bright pink. Since they are not flowers, the display lasts months.

In the wild, bougainvillea climbs up trees and bushes in forests. Plants that grow in this way are known as vines, and like many vines, bougainvillea has sharp thorns that hook onto branches to give it a firm grip. Today, you will often find bougainvillea climbing over balconies and porches, and around the walls and arches of courtyards. It needs plenty of sunshine, or its colors may fade, and it also hates frost, so it grows best in warm climates.

Great bougainvillea
(*Bougainvillea spectabilis*)
Originally from Brazil, bougainvillea can be seen climbing up buildings and walls in many warm countries.

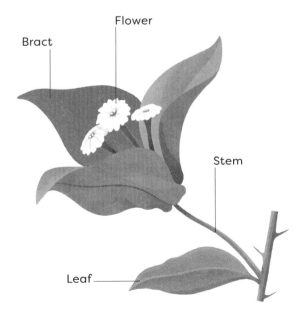

Bract
Flower
Stem
Leaf

Two types of leaf

Bougainvillea has ordinary green leaves as well as special pink leaves, or bracts. The bracts are arranged in bunches, with several tiny white flowers in the middle. Sometimes, the flowers are almost completely hidden by the much larger bracts.

45

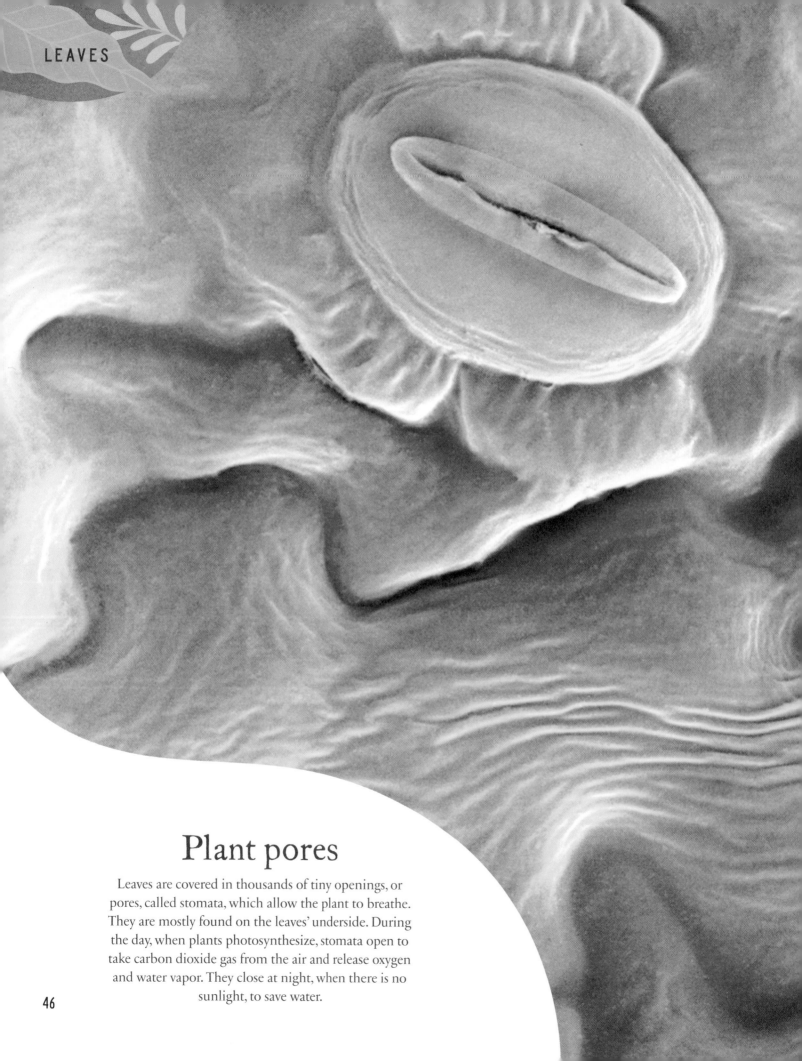

Plant pores

Leaves are covered in thousands of tiny openings, or pores, called stomata, which allow the plant to breathe. They are mostly found on the leaves' underside. During the day, when plants photosynthesize, stomata open to take carbon dioxide gas from the air and release oxygen and water vapor. They close at night, when there is no sunlight, to save water.

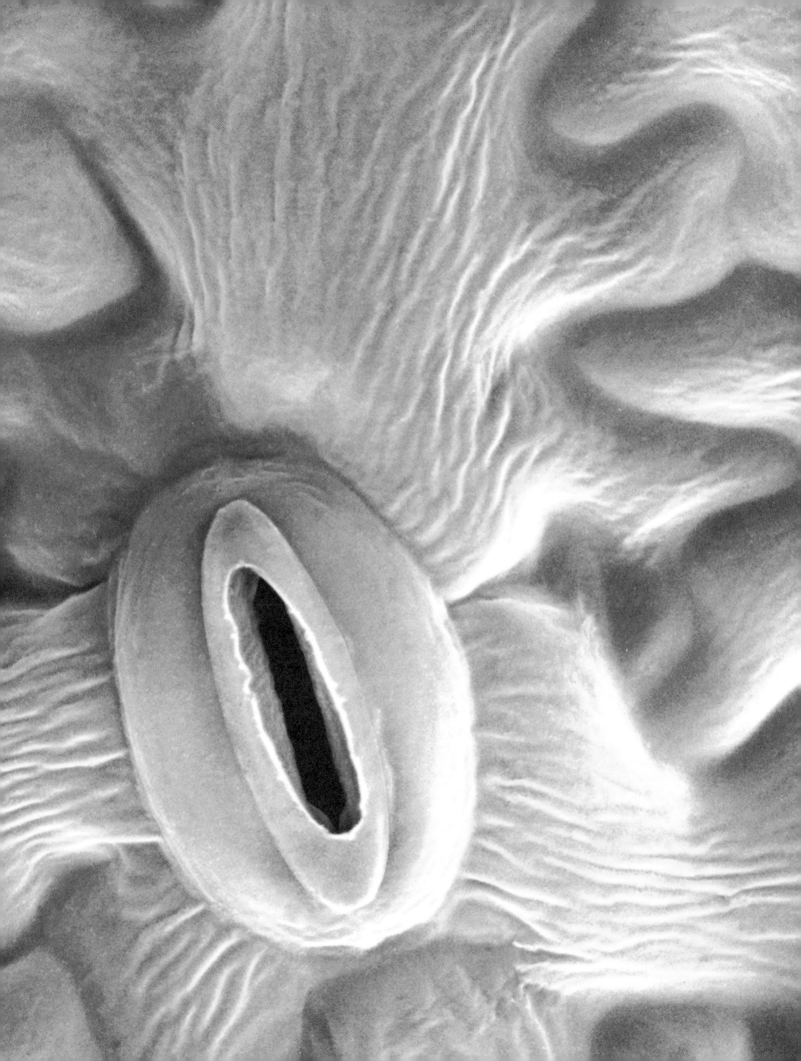

CHAPTER 2

Stems and trunks

Stems link the different parts of plants. They connect the roots with the leaves, flowers, and fruits, and hold them all in place. Most stems grow upward toward the light, while others creep over the ground, cling to things, or tunnel through soil. Some plants use stems to store water or food. Trees have hard stems called trunks, with layers of strong wood inside and bark on the outside.

Strong stem
The hollow stems are strengthened by the mineral silica. This is what makes the stem feel rough to the touch.

The rough horsetail can reach 3 ft (1 m) high.

Small, black leaves form a ring around the stem joint.

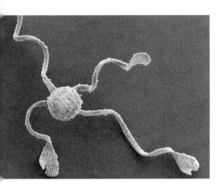

Springy spore
A horsetail spore has four whiplike extensions. These curl and uncurl depending on the weather to make the spore move! The spore wriggles or bounces along until ready to grow.

Stem joints
The horsetail stem has many segments. Pointed leaves grow at the joints between the sections.

The stem is ridged and feels very rough.

Horsetail

Horsetails use their strong, green stems to capture all the sunlight they need.

In the marshes and swamps of the northern parts of the world, you might come across certain strange plants in boggy ground. They grow in clumps, and seem to be all stem. These are horsetails. Their stems are straight and apparently bare, with no leaves. If you take a closer look, however, you will see every stem has black rings around it—these are clusters of minuscule leaves. The odd leaves of horsetails are tiny and dark, almost like hair, so are no use to gather sunlight. Instead, horsetails photosynthesize with their stems, which are green with chlorophyll. Having small leaves doesn't hold horsetails back, though—they spread quickly, covering large areas.

In the distant past, some horsetails were enormous. These mega-horsetails included Calamites, which lived over 300 million years ago and grew as tall as a 15-story building. When these ancient plants died, they added to the deposits of coal that were slowly forming. The giant horsetails went extinct long ago, but the coal they left behind has been used as a fuel for hundreds of years.

Rough horsetail
(Equisetum hyemale)
This horsetail lives in cool parts of northern Asia, Europe, and North America. Its dried stems can be used for polishing and as sandpaper.

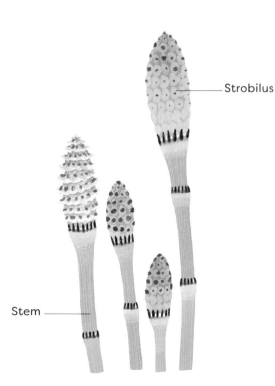

Strobilus

Stem

Stems with spores
Horsetails spread not with seeds but with microscopic spores. The plant produces a lumpy structure, called a strobilus, at the top of some stems. This contains the spores, which spring from the strobilus in dry weather and are carried away on the breeze.

Pampas grass leaves have such sharp edges they can draw blood!

Taller, leafless stems carry flower spikes at the top.

Long, sharp-edged leaves develop from the stems.

The stems are tall and rodlike.

Feathery flowers

The whitish flower spikes of pampas grass are the tallest part of the plant. They produce millions of pollen grains. The masses of airborne pollen made by grasses can give people hay fever.

Tough but flexible

Pampas grass has tough stems that sway in the wind without bending or snapping.

Pampas grass

The monster flower stalks of this grass seem to be giant feathers stuck in the ground.

We often pay little attention to grasses, but there is much more to these amazing plants than most people realize. There are thousands of different grasses, not all of which are small and green, and they thrive all over the planet, from the Arctic to the edges of Antarctica. Grasses cover over a fifth of the Earth's land. You find the largest grasslands in areas too wet to be desert but too dry to be forest. One such place is the pampas, which is a vast, windy plain in the south of South America. This is the home of pampas grass, a towering species that reaches 10 ft (3 m) tall.

Pampas grass has three winning features, which are shared by every species in the grass family. First, the growing points of its leaves are down at the base, and thereby survive their upper parts being nibbled by grazing animals, and being burnt by wildfires. Second, it has a dense network of roots that easily send up new stems. Third, it uses the wind to disperse masses of its pollen and seeds over wide areas, so it spreads quickly.

Pampas grass
(Cortaderia selloana)
Clumps of this grass are a familiar sight in parks and gardens. It is originally from the pampas grasslands of southern South America.

From the ground up
Unlike most plants, the growing point of grass stems is at soil level, not at the tip. Therefore, if a grass is cut, this does not kill it—it simply keeps pushing up from the ground. This is why grassy lawns can be mown regularly.

Bamboo

The woody stems of bamboo are extremely strong and fast-growing.

On mountains in China there are magical forests that soar high above your head, yet have no trees. These are forests of bamboo, the largest kind of grass. Bamboo grows faster than any other plant on Earth. The stems of giant timber bamboo are able to grow over 35 in (90 cm) a day! How does this grass grow so rapidly? The answer is that bamboo is very efficient. Its stems power straight upward and do not waste energy producing leaves until they are already tall. All of the energy they need to do this comes from their parent plant, which they are connected to underground. Bamboo stems are also thin for their height. Rather than becoming thicker with age, like trees do, they put everything they have into vertical growth. Some giant timber bamboo is 66 ft (20 m) tall!

In China, Japan, and parts of southern Asia, bamboo is harvested on a large scale. The sturdy stems are ideal for ladders and building construction—it is even used to make scaffolding for soaring skyscrapers. Tough fibers extracted from bamboo can also be used to make clothes.

Giant timber bamboo
(*Phyllostachys bambusoides*)
In the wild, this bamboo lives in China. It is planted as a crop in several Asian countries.

Bamboo shoots
Part of a bamboo's stem is underground and runs sideways through the soil. Buds on this stem send up new shoots, which look like small spears. The young shoots of some bamboo species are picked as a vegetable, but they must be cooked to make them edible.

Growing

Harvested

Hollow stem

The stems of giant timber bamboo are hollow. This is useful because people can use them as pipes to get water to fields and homes.

There are joints at regular intervals along the stem, which strengthen it.

Bamboo rarely flowers, but when it does, it usually dies afterward.

Mineral support

Bamboo stems contain high levels of silica, the mineral from which much of the world's sand is made. The silica makes the stems strong, so they can grow tall even without a woody trunk.

Eating bamboo

Giant pandas, whose main food is bamboo, have six digits on their front paws to grip the stalks firmly.

Some varieties of bamboo have stems and leaves of more than one color.

Bamboo stems have a beautiful glossy surface.

Living stone

Living stones, also called pebble plants, have virtually no stem. They live in the deserts of southern Africa and consist of two fat leaves that look just like real stones. It's the perfect disguise because they hide the plants from leaf-eating animals—except when they burst into flower.

Hairy spines

At the base of each cluster of spines is a fuzzy blob of fibers. The cactus flowers grow from these fiberous blobs.

The stem is folded into about 30 ribs, which help shade the plant.

Shallow roots

The roots of the barrel cactus grow near the surface and reach outward a long way from the plant to soak up precious rain and dew as fast as possible. Fine hairs on the roots help them absorb water.

Storage cells

Inside the cactus stem, there are many special water-storage cells. These can quickly expand or shrink as needed.

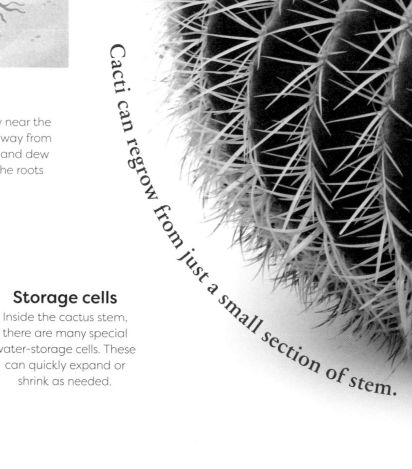

Cacti can regrow from just a small section of stem.

Barrel cactus

The spines are actually hard, pointy leaves. They are arranged in neat lines along the ribs.

Cacti fill their enormously fat stems with water to survive in deserts.

Touching a cactus is a painful mistake you won't want to repeat. Cacti are the hedgehogs of the plant world, with spiky stems that bristle with hundreds of sharp spines. It's an excellent defense against being munched by animals, but it is not just for food that animals are drawn to cacti. Most of these plants live in the sandy, stony deserts of North, Central, and South America, where water is very hard to find—and thirsty creatures know that cacti are full of water. During rare desert thunderstorms, cacti stems expand massively to store every last drop of rain. Barrel cacti have ribs on their stems that open out like pleats in a skirt to give them maximum stretch. The ribs also channel dew, which forms during the cold desert nights, down to the roots.

Cacti spines can be straight like needles or curved like hooks, depending on the species. Those of the golden barrel cactus grow in star-shaped clusters. As well as providing defense, the spines shade the vulnerable fleshy stem from the scorching desert sun.

Golden barrel cactus
(Echinocactus grusonii)
The golden barrel cactus is an endangered species that lives on a few rocky hillsides in Mexico.

59

Plant defenses

Plants are excellent at self-defense. After all, unlike animals, they can't run away from something that wants to eat them. They often arm themselves with weapons such as spines, thorns, and stinging hairs. Plants can also flood their sap, leaves, and fruit with toxic chemicals.

Poison tree

The white sap of this plant from southern Africa—which is not a real tree—can cause blindness. The San people used to dip their arrows in the sap when they went hunting.

Poison ivy

Poison ivy is one of the most feared plants in North America. Anyone who comes into contact with this climbing plant's milky sap risks getting an itchy rash.

Common milkweed

Milkweed contains unpleasant toxins, but this does not put off the caterpillars of monarch butterflies. They absorb the toxins into their bodies to use as their own defense.

Castor bean

The seeds of the castor oil plant, which look like beans, are coated with ricin. This deadly substance is one of the world's most dangerous poisons.

Stinging tree

This Australian plant is like a stinging nettle the size of a tree. It has needlelike hairs that inject a toxin so powerful, the pain lasts for days.

Ant plant

The stems of this plant swell up and turn hollow. Stinging ants move into the hollows, and in return for their home, they defend the plant from leaf-munching insects.

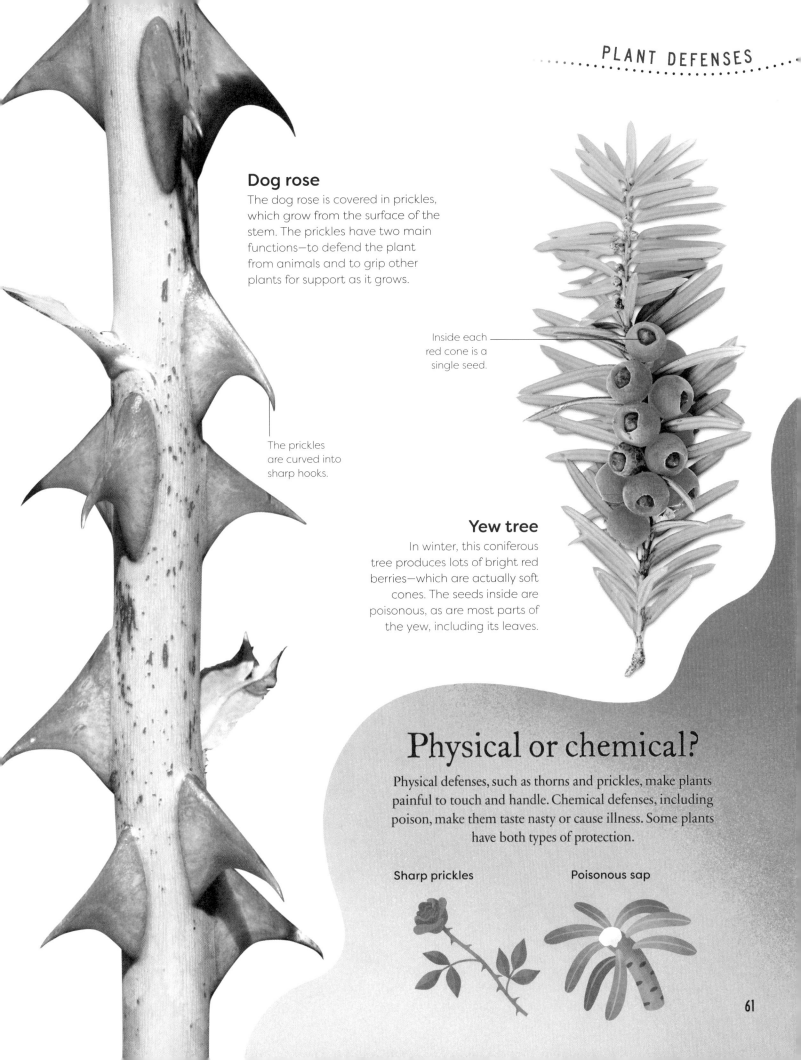

Dog rose

The dog rose is covered in prickles, which grow from the surface of the stem. The prickles have two main functions—to defend the plant from animals and to grip other plants for support as it grows.

The prickles are curved into sharp hooks.

Inside each red cone is a single seed.

Yew tree

In winter, this coniferous tree produces lots of bright red berries—which are actually soft cones. The seeds inside are poisonous, as are most parts of the yew, including its leaves.

Physical or chemical?

Physical defenses, such as thorns and prickles, make plants painful to touch and handle. Chemical defenses, including poison, make them taste nasty or cause illness. Some plants have both types of protection.

Sharp prickles

Poisonous sap

61

Right-handed plants

Sweet peas are sometimes called right-handed, because their tendrils always curl to the right. Other plants, such as hedge bindweed, are left-handed.

Sweet peas live just one year, so must be resown in spring.

Tendrils reach out from the ends of branches, which split off from the main stem.

The petals of developing flowers are green at first.

Sweet pea
(Lathyrus odoratus)

The sweet peas we grow usually have pink, purple, blue, or white flowers. Their wild ancestor, which lives in Italy, is always purple.

Hooked tendril

The tendrils of sweet peas are thin and wiry, with pointed tips that catch on nearby objects.

Sweet pea

**Sweet peas have special
stems that twirl in the air to
find things to cling to.**

A gorgeous scent drifts across gardens and balconies in summer.
It belongs to sweet pea flowers. Sweet peas are known as climbing
plants, or climbers, because of the unusual way they grow up toward
the light. Sweet pea stems are unable to support themselves—
without help they would flop over—so they borrow the sturdier
stems of other plants by grabbing onto them. Plants can't see,
though, so how do the sweet peas know where these supports are?
They have the perfect solution. At the ends of their branches, they
grow curly tendrils, which twirl around until they find something
they can hold onto. The movement is too slow for us to see, unless
we record it and speed up the film. When the tendrils touch another
object, they wrap around and around it in a neat coil to
hold the stem secure.

Sweet peas belong to the pea family, which includes garden peas,
chickpeas, and beans. Many of these plants are important crops,
but sweet peas are not edible. They are grown just for
the joy that their colors and perfume bring.

Tendrils move

Tendrils wrap
around support

New tendrils
move

Finding support

Sweet peas tendrils extend away
from the plant. They slowly move in
circles as they grow, like someone
swinging a rope around their head.
When they touch an object, they
twist around it. In gardens, people
provide supports for the plants.

63

Red river gum

The bark on gum trees is always peeling. This produces beautiful patterns on their trunks.

Many places in the world are associated with a particular type of tree. Australia is the land of gum, or eucalyptus, trees. More than three-quarters of its trees are gum trees, and they form huge forests. Most gums have handsome evergreen leaves, which are often silvery or bluish. However, it is their extraordinary bark that really makes them stand out. Unlike other trees, which hold onto their bark for a long time, gum trees replace theirs each year. As the old bark comes away from the trunk, it reveals a new layer underneath. The layers look different, and this creates eye-catching patterns. In red river gums, there can be patches of gray, brown, pink, and orange.

Bark is vital to trees because it stops them from drying out and protects them from extreme heat and cold. It also defends them from attack by fungi and insects. But if bark is so important, why do gum trees keep changing it? Maybe this keeps the bark in good condition, or perhaps it allows the tree's trunk to grow fatter —no one knows for sure.

Red river gum
(Eucalyptus camaldulensis)
Red river gums are unique to Australia. They grow beside rivers and small lakes, and on floodplains.

64

Blistered and cracked bark is a sign of a healthy gum tree.

Dry river

Many Australian rivers dry up for months on end. This photograph, taken from the air, shows lines of red river gums along the banks of a dry riverbed.

Hollow homes

Hollows in the trunks of gum trees are homes for parrots and small mammals called possums. Bearlike koalas snooze in their branches.

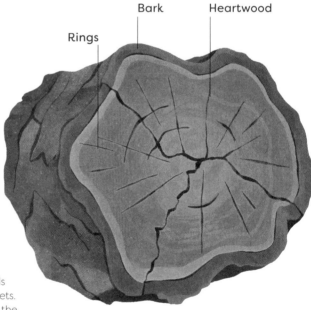

Rings

Bark

Heartwood

The old bark peels off in strips or sheets. These hang from the trunk, then drop to the ground.

Red wood

At the center of every tree trunk is the heartwood, which in red river gums is blood-red. Trees usually add a new ring of heartwood each year, so by counting the rings you can tell how old the tree is.

65

Dazzling bark

The rainbow eucalyptus has the most colorful trunk of any tree. Its outer bark peels away to reveal a bright green inner layer. This gradually changes color as it ages. Many dazzling shades appear, depending on how long each area of bark has been exposed to the air.

Small seeds

Despite their great size, giant sequoias grow from seeds the size of grains of rice. Their cones would fit in the palm of your hand.

The red bark is soft and spongy, and up to 24 in (60 cm) thick.

An old sequoia has up to 50,000 seeds in all its cones combined.

Giant sequoia
(Sequoiadendron giganteum)

Giant sequoias once grew in much of North America and Europe. Today, they live only in the Sierra Nevada Mountains in California—some are 3,000 years old.

Deep grooves run up and down the trunk.

Tallest tree

While giant sequoias are the heaviest trees in the world, coastal redwoods are the tallest. One, known as "Hyperion," measures about 377 ft (115 m)!

Giant sequoia

Thanks to their colossal trunks, giant sequoias are among the tallest trees on the planet.

You will get a sore neck if you stand at the foot of a giant sequoia and stare up at the top. These trees tower over the forest floor in California. For them to reach a height of 250 ft (75 m) is not unusual. Some keep growing past 330 ft (100 m), so are as high as a soccer field is long. Two close relatives of the giant sequoia, known as redwoods for their rust-colored bark, also grow to enormous heights. It would be impossible to grow much taller, because their trunks simply could not transport water any higher.

Giant sequoias are conifers, with scaly, evergreen leaves and cones full of seeds. We know from the rings in their trunks—which, like all trees, usually add one ring of growth a year—that they may live thousands of years. They can survive wildfires, due to their shield of thick bark. However, climate change is making the fires larger and more intense, so will they still be able to cope? It would be a terrible loss if one day the climate became too tough for these awesome trees and they died out.

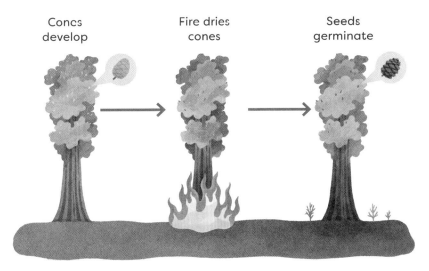

Concs develop → Fire dries cones → Seeds germinate

Helped by fire

The cones of giant sequoias take around two years to mature. During a wildfire, heat dries the ripe cones, so they split and drop their seeds. Ash from the fire is fertilizer for the seedlings, which thrive in the burned-out clearings.

Mighty mower
The leaves and twigs of Arctic willows are a favorite food of the huge musk ox, which browses on them year-round.

This tree only grows during the brief Arctic summer.

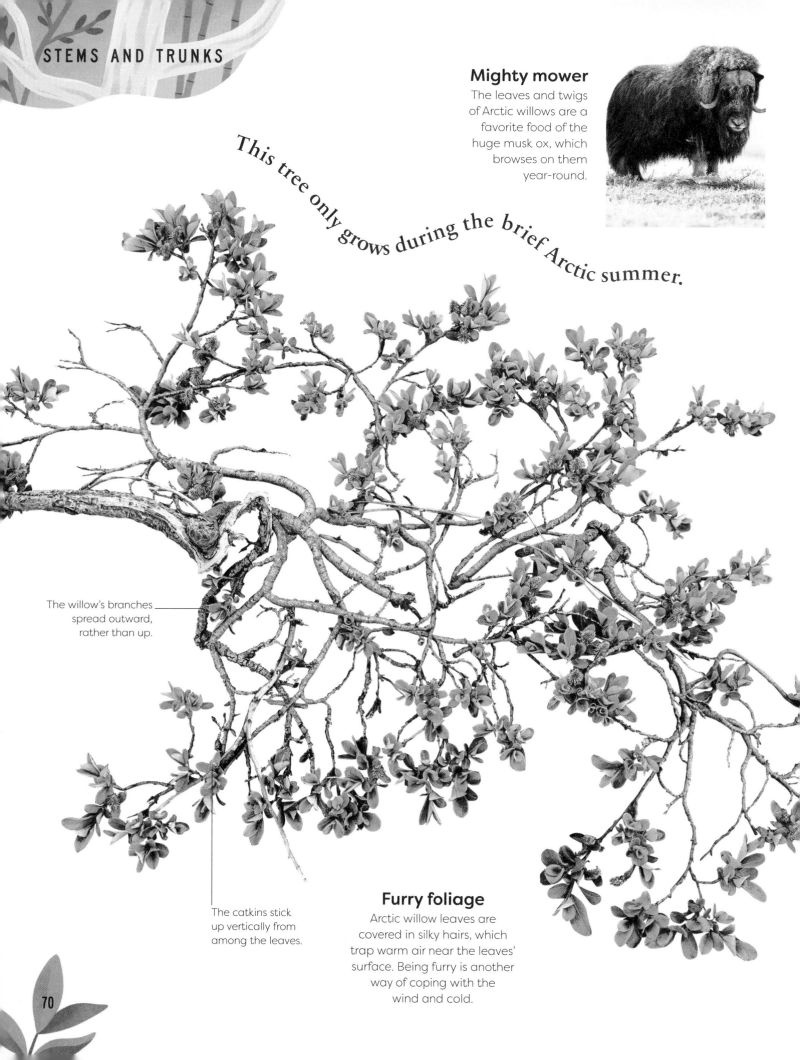

The willow's branches spread outward, rather than up.

The catkins stick up vertically from among the leaves.

Furry foliage
Arctic willow leaves are covered in silky hairs, which trap warm air near the leaves' surface. Being furry is another way of coping with the wind and cold.

Arctic willow

The Arctic willow lacks a trunk and is one of the shortest trees in the world.

Height is a serious disadvantage in the Arctic. Howling winds blast across the wild, open landscape, known as tundra, and would immediately uproot and topple tall trees. The Arctic willow copes with life in this extremely windy place by doing without a trunk. It grows sideways over the ground, out of the wind. Its highest leaves rise only a few inches above the surrounding moss and stones, so if you went on a stroll across the tundra, you would actually be walking on top of these trees! Tundra soil is low in nutrients and for long periods the land is shrouded in darkness, so the willow creeps along very slowly.

Down at ground level, the Arctic willow traps warm, moist air between its low-growing branches. This means the tree creates its own microclimate, which is noticeably warmer and damper than the air above. The snug conditions suit a variety of other small plants that flourish next to the willow. In turn, these plants and the willow are food for many animals, including mouselike lemmings, Arctic hares, and herds of reindeer.

Arctic willow
(Salix arctica)
This miniature tree is found throughout the Arctic tundra. Farther south, the Arctic willow lives in high mountains, where the climate is almost as tough.

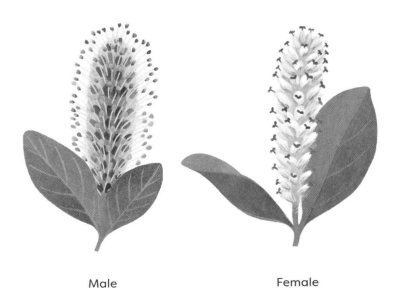

Male

Female

Colorful catkins

In summer, the Arctic willow is covered in fluffy bundles that look like small sticks of candyfloss. These are catkins and they contain the willow flowers, which are yellowish in male trees and red in female trees. Tiny flies pollinate them.

71

Norway spruce

These conifers are grown for their timber, which is used to make paper pulp and cardboard. They are also felled when they are young to be used as Christmas trees.

Rattan canes have long spines for protection.

Rings in the heartwood show the age of the tree.

Rattan

This strong, vinelike palm is harvested from the wild in Asia's rain forests. The tough stems, called canes, can be woven into furniture or used in handicrafts.

Animal architects

Many animals rely on trees for building materials, just like humans. Birds weave nests from sticks and leaves, wasps chew strips of wood to make paper for their nests, and beavers pull trunks and branches across rivers to form dams.

Bird nest

Wasp nest

Beaver dam

72

Made from trees

Trees make our world go round. They give us thousands of different products, from foods and drinks to building materials and life-changing medicines. Some items are taken from living trees, while others require the trees to be cut down. Planting new trees ensures a future harvest.

Balsa tree

Balsa tree trunks have less woody material than other trees, so they grow very fast. The light wood is perfect for model-making and was once used for aircraft bodies.

Rubber tree

Rubber comes from the milky sap of rubber trees. It is naturally white, but turns black when chemicals are added to create the material we use in tires and shoe soles.

Cork oak

The outer bark of this tree is waterproof. It is removed in layers, without damaging the inner bark, then is turned into cork bottle stoppers and floor tiles.

Oil palm

The red fruit of oil palms are made into palm oil. This goes into many groceries, such as sauces, peanut butter, and soap. Some rain forests are cut down to grow oil palms.

Quinine

The bark of this South American tree is the source of a drug called quinine. It is given as a medicine to people with malaria, a terrible disease that has killed millions worldwide.

Tagua nut tree

Tagua nuts have several fat seeds inside. They contain a hard, white substance known as vegetable ivory, which can be carved into jewelry and ornaments.

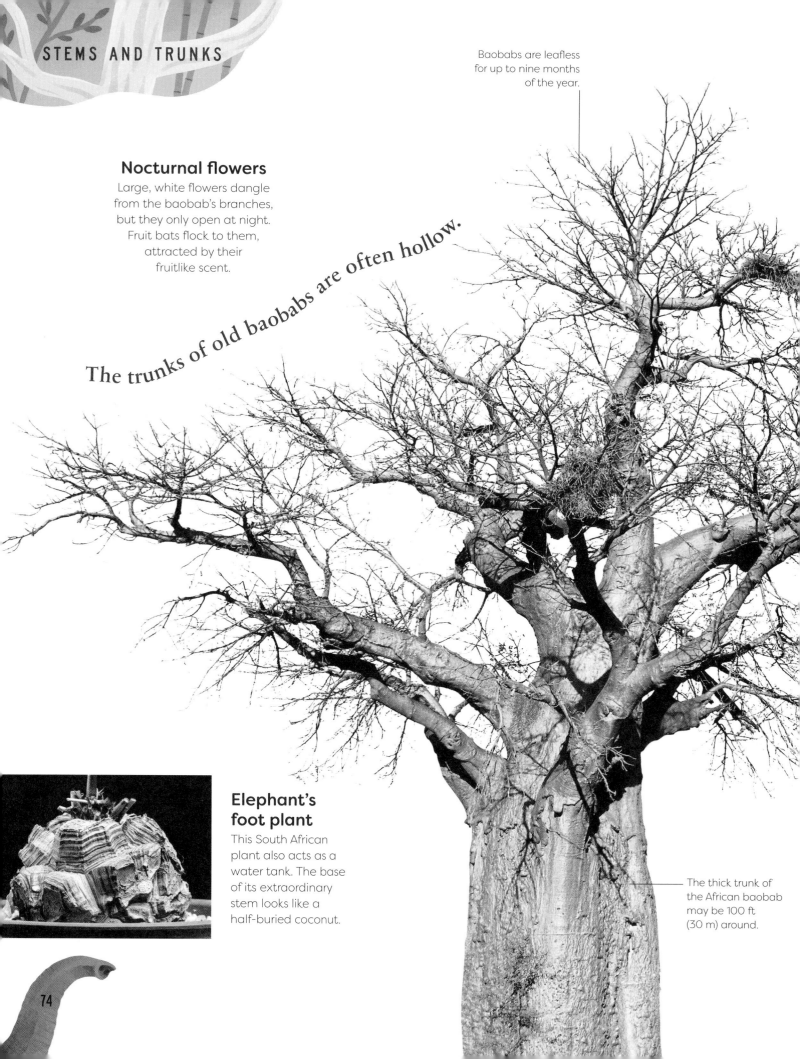

Baobabs are leafless
for up to nine months
of the year.

Nocturnal flowers

Large, white flowers dangle
from the baobab's branches,
but they only open at night.
Fruit bats flock to them,
attracted by their
fruitlike scent.

The trunks of old baobabs are often hollow.

Elephant's foot plant

This South African
plant also acts as a
water tank. The base
of its extraordinary
stem looks like a
half-buried coconut.

The thick trunk of
the African baobab
may be 100 ft
(30 m) around.

Baobab

These trees develop gigantic, tubby trunks, and the shade they provide is a welcome relief in the hot savanna.

Many baobabs survive for 1,000 to 1,500 years, and with the passage of time, their trunk becomes wider and wider. One famous old baobab in South Africa measures 154 ft (47 m) around its trunk! To give the tree a hug, you would probably need 25 adults holding hands in a circle. Ancient baobabs like this can be seen from afar in Africa's grasslands. The wildlife that lives there naturally heads toward them, because these trees often grow where there is a reliable source of freshwater.

The trunk of a baobab swells like a sponge as it takes on thousands of gallons of water. During periods of drought, it shrinks again. With its wide, swollen trunk, the bare branches above seem rather small and puny by comparison. Legend says that the baobab was turned upside-down by a god, and ended up with its roots in the air, as punishment for bad behavior. Many parts of the African baobab are useful—its leaves, seeds, and the pulp of its fruits are all cooked and eaten, and a red dye can be made from its roots.

African baobab
(Adansonia digitata)
There are eight types of baobabs. The African baobab lives in central Africa and western Asia.

Water stealers
Thirsty elephants tear at the bark of baobabs to get at the damp inner wood. However, the trees heal themselves by creating new bark, which seals the wounds. Many baobab trunks bear the scars of past elephant attacks.

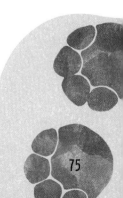

The leaves are torched in fires but quickly regrow.

The grass tree is distantly related to lilies.

Young grass trees have an upright spray of leaves. As the trees age, the leaves make a ball shape.

Growing tip

The growing tip of the grass tree is surrounded by its leaves. They cover it up, protecting it from blazes.

Inside the trunk

The trunk's outer layer consists of dead leaf bases stuck together with a kind of natural glue. Only the spongy part in the middle is alive.

Each year, the trunk grows just 1 in (2 cm) taller.

76

Grass tree

Neither a grass or a tree, this peculiar plant has a black trunk scorched by fire.

Away from the coast, much of Australia is baked by hot sun and looks like a sea of sand. It hardly ever rains and the fine, dusty earth has few nutrients. Barely any trees grow here. Instead, the land is covered in a dense tangle of bushes. Among them is the grass tree. With its fat trunk and tuft of long, thin leaves, you can see how the plant earned its name. However, its trunk is not like those of real trees. The center is soft, rather than woody. The surface appears to be bark, but isn't. It's actually a thick layer of padding made from the bottom part of old leaves.

The grass tree's unusual trunk is fireproof, which is a lifesaver because huge wildfires are common in this dry landscape. Fierce flames char the trunk, but do no real harm. The living part is safe inside, and the grass tree survives. In fact, it depends on fire—flames cause it to flower. The leafy jacket provides such good protection that grass trees can live for up to 450 years.

Grass tree
(Xanthorrhoea australis)
The grass tree is found only in the south and west of Australia. It lives in sandy habitats and grows up to 10 ft (3 m) high.

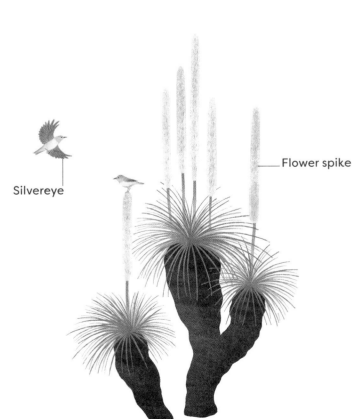

Silvereye

Flower spike

Fire flowers

As vegetation burns, it releases ethene gas. When the grass tree detects this, it sends up a giant flower spike, which contains thousands of tiny blooms. Small birds called silvereyes visit to sip the nectar, and at the same time spread the pollen between different grass trees.

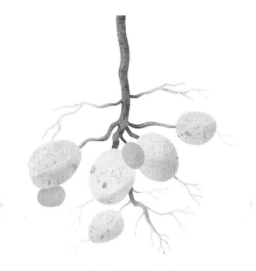

CHAPTER 3

Roots and bulbs

Roots are amazing. They spread through the soil to form huge networks that anchor plants firmly. Fine hairs on them act like thousands of straws, all sucking up water and nutrients for the plants to use. Some roots have even moved above ground and become strong to help support trees. Many plants keep supplies of food in their roots too, or in other underground stores.

Air plants flower only once and die soon after.

Fuzzy leaves

The leaves of air plants can appear silvery and fuzzy due to their covering of spongelike cells for collecting water.

When the sky plant is ready to flower, its leaves turn pink or red.

The sky plant's roots grip whatever it is growing on.

Growing anywhere

Air plants will happily live anywhere in midair—even on overhead wires! Indoors, people often display them on pieces of shell or stone.

Air plant

Air plants can grow without soil and their roots attach to almost any surface.

Growing in nothing but air may seem impossible, but not for air plants. These extraordinary organisms have no need for any kind of soil. They are able to survive when suspended in midair on tree branches or rocks. Their weird leaves might remind you of tentacles, and their roots are strange too, because they're not much use at absorbing water and essential minerals—which is what roots usually do. So how do air plants survive? Their leaves take what they need from the air directly. Mist, clouds, and rain give them water to drink, and there are enough nutrients dissolved in it for them to live on. The air plants' tangled, wiry roots are used instead to secure them to whichever support they are growing on.

Plants that don't grow in the ground are called epiphytes. Many are found in the treetops of tropical forests. Branches can be covered in so many of these plants, they look like colorful sky gardens. The pools of water that gather at the center of large epiphytes are used as ponds by tiny tree frogs!

Sky plant
(Tillandsia ionantha)
There are hundreds of different air plants in Central and South America, including the handsome sky plant. This species is a popular house plant.

Soaking up water

Releasing water

Absorbing water
The surface of every air plant leaf has many tiny structures, called trichomes. When droplets of water fall on a trichome, it soaks them up like a miniature sponge. The trichome fills with water, then empties its contents into the leaf below.

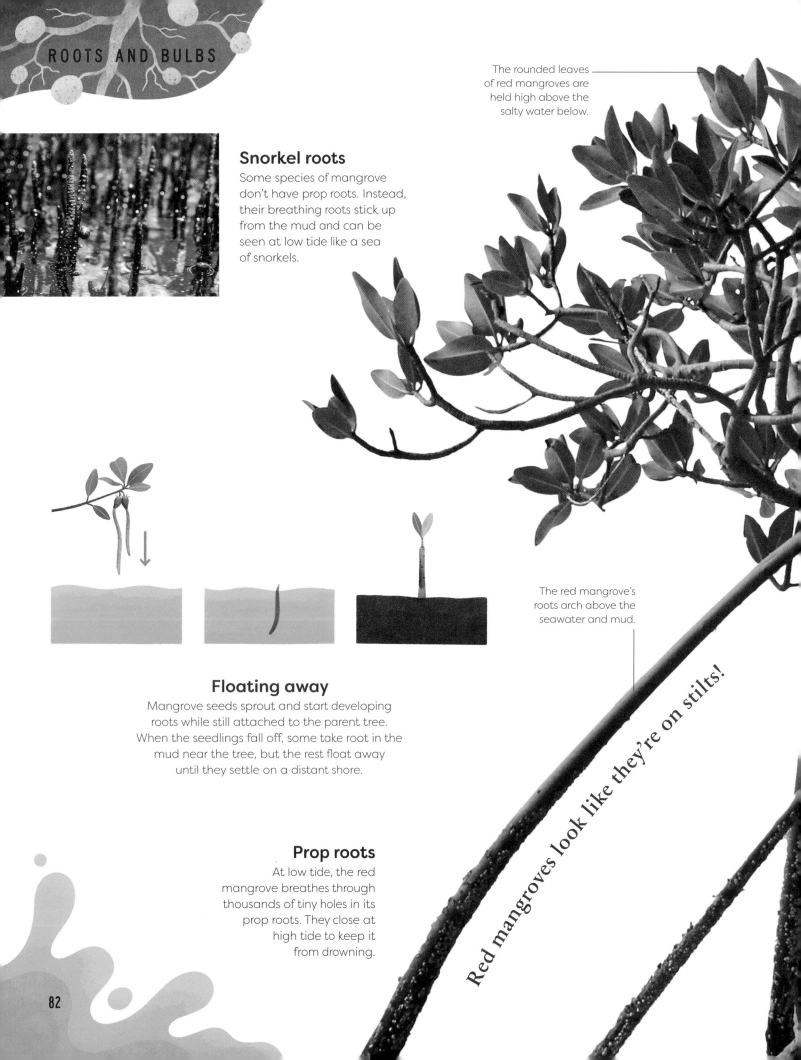

The rounded leaves of red mangroves are held high above the salty water below.

Snorkel roots

Some species of mangrove don't have prop roots. Instead, their breathing roots stick up from the mud and can be seen at low tide like a sea of snorkels.

Floating away

Mangrove seeds sprout and start developing roots while still attached to the parent tree. When the seedlings fall off, some take root in the mud near the tree, but the rest float away until they settle on a distant shore.

Prop roots

At low tide, the red mangrove breathes through thousands of tiny holes in its prop roots. They close at high tide to keep it from drowning.

The red mangrove's roots arch above the seawater and mud.

Red mangroves look like they're on stilts!

Mangrove

Mangrove roots thrive in saltwater, so these trees can form forests along the seashore.

Too much salt kills plants, which is why trees normally don't live in the sea. Plants on the coast must also cope with the never-ending movement of tides. Twice a day, the sea rushes in and floods the shore, then drains away. Mangroves love it here, though. Red mangroves use their gangly roots to prop up their trunk, so their branches and leaves are clear of the water. When the incoming tide covers the roots, they drink the seawater and filter out the dangerous salt. While the tide is out, the roots are exposed to the air and can breathe in oxygen. Other species of mangrove get rid of extra salt through their leaves. If you looked closely, you'd even see they were covered in its white crystals!

Mangrove forests are a safe nursery for young fish and turtles. The maze of roots shelters them from large predators. Mangroves also protect many towns and villages from the sea. Their roots defend the coast by holding back the waves during violent storms, and prevent sand and soil from being washed away.

Red mangrove
(Rhizophora mangle)
Forests of red mangroves can be seen along many tropical coasts, especially on both sides of the Atlantic Ocean.

Strangler figs can cover up buildings and hide them.

Many forest animals live among the strangler fig leaves.

A strangler fig has what look like branches, but these are actually roots.

Inside the fig

If a host tree dies and rots away, the strangler fig remains as a hollow column. It may be large enough for several people to stand inside!

Root network

Hundreds of roots join up to form a giant network. They may belong to several strangler figs, all wrapped around the same tree.

84

Strangler fig

These plants wrap entire
trees in their ropelike roots,
and may even kill them.

Tropical rain forests are bursting with life. So many plants live here,
that they must fight for space and light. Strangler figs have a neat
solution to the problem of how to survive in such a crowded place.
They take over other trees. Every strangler fig begins life on a branch
high in the treetops, after its seed was left behind in the poo of a bird
or mammal. The fig seedling is unusual, because it has woody roots
that have to grow toward the ground far below. More and more roots
coil around the outside of the tree trunk as the seedling gets bigger
and sends out leaves. Strangler figs cover their host tree with so many
of their own leaves and roots, and suck so many minerals out of the
earth, that the tree is starved of sunlight and food, and can die. Even
though strangler figs kill trees, they are important to rain forests.
Their fruit—juicy figs—are a feast for parrots, orangutans,
monkeys, and many more.

Strangler fig
(Ficus)
Many types of figs that
live in the world's tropical
forests are strangler figs. In
some countries, their roots
grow over the ruins of
ancient cities.

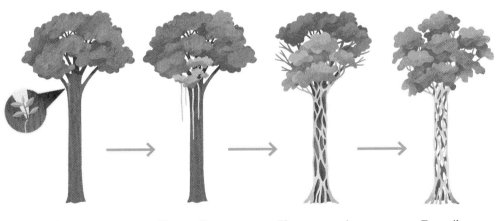

Tree

Fig sapling
sprouts

Fig surrounds
tree

Tree dies

Tree takeover

A strangler fig sends its roots
down a tree from the top.
The roots can surround the trunk
completely to reach the ground.
If the tree dies, all that's left is
the tower of fig roots, with the
fig's leaves at the top.

Cassava

Millions of people worldwide eat this chunky root vegetable, which is packed with energy.

Every day, much of the planet's population tucks into at least one meal that includes plant roots or underground stems, commonly known as root vegetables. These vegetables have plenty of carbohydrates, one of the main sources of energy for the human body. They include potatoes, yams, sweet potatoes, and cassava. Cassava, also called manioc, is the huge brown root of the cassava plant. It can't be eaten raw—it has to go through many processes in order to make it safe, including being peeled, chopped, soaked, and cooked—but it is very popular. Today, up to 500 million people in Africa depend on cassava, as well as millions more in Asia, and Central and South America.

Cassava is a superfood because a field of it gives us more food energy than the same size of field planted with any other crop. It does not need fertilizer, and can even be grown in poor-quality soil that lacks nutrients. Archaeologists think cassava was first planted as a crop in Central America over 8,000 years ago. The people that grew it were some of the earliest farmers.

Cassava
(Manihot esculenta)
Fields of cassava are a familiar sight in many tropical regions. The main variety grown today originally came from Brazil.

Roots or stems?
As they mature, cassava plants begin to store food and water in their roots, which fatten up in bunches in the soil. Potatoes look similar, but they are in fact massively swollen stems that grow underground at the base of the potato plant.

Cassava

Potato

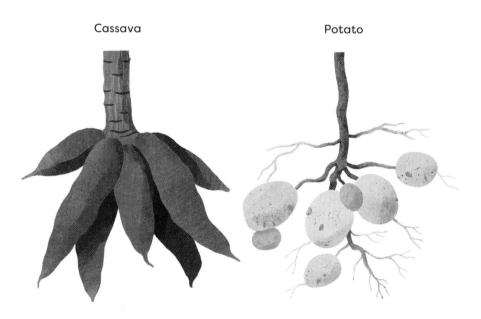

The root is an emergency food store for the cassava plant.

Poison danger

Raw cassava roots are poisonous! Their flesh contains cyanide, a deadly chemical that can kill people, but careful preparation makes them edible. The poison is a chemical defense against herbivores and germs.

Cassava flour is used to make bread and cakes.

Fat cassava roots, or tubers, have a tough, brown covering.

The pointed end grows downward.

Starch store

When harvested, the white flesh of cassava is two-fifths starch, a type of carbohydrate that gives us energy. The rest is water.

Flavorings

We use different parts of plants to change how our food and drink tastes and looks. Animals don't do this, only people. Early humans were adding peppery seeds to fish and meat as long as 6,000 years ago!

Saffron

This expensive spice is from the saffron crocus. The stigmas, a female part of the flower, are collected by hand. It takes 150,000 crocuses to make just 2 lb (1 kg) of saffron.

Garlic

Bulbs of garlic grow underground. Each has a papery wrapper inside which there are tightly packed segments called cloves. Chopping garlic gives off its powerful aroma and flavor.

Ginger

Wild ginger grows in forests in southern Asia, although the spice comes from cultivated varieties. Their underground stems look like lumpy potatoes, and are used in many Asian dishes and cakes.

Cilantro

Cilantro is often sold in big bunches. Its frilly leaves are used as an herb, while its dried seeds, called coriander, are used as a spice. Cuisines around the world wouldn't be the same without it!

Cinnamon

Most bark looks inedible, yet we actually eat the bark of several trees. Cinnamon is the inner layer of bark of the cinnamon tree, from southern Asia.

Be careful not to touch a chilli pepper and then touch your eyes—it will hurt.

Chili pepper

Chili peppers are used worldwide, but these fruits originally come from South America. Their hot taste is caused by a chemical, capsaicin, that activates heat sensors in our mouth.

Sugarcane

Most sugar comes from grass! Sugarcane is a tall grass grown in Brazil, India, and other tropical countries. Its stalks are mashed to release sweet sap, which is then dried to make sugar crystals.

Vanilla

Vanilla comes from an orchid that grows on forest trees. Its dangling seedpods give us the flavor we love. However, wild vanilla is costly to produce, so today scientists make imitation vanilla in labs.

The seedpod of a vanilla orchid is dried before the seeds are removed to use as flavoring.

Herb or spice?

An herb is usually a fresh green leaf, but a spice is often dried before use and comes from any plant part, including seeds, fruits, flowers, and bark. Spices are often ground to a powder or crushed to release their smell and flavor.

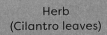

Herb
(Cilantro leaves)

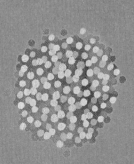

Spice
(Coriander seeds)

Clover

Clover roots are able to capture nitrogen from the air with a little help from tiny bacteria.

A lawn or meadow often has plants other than grass. Among them is clover, which has leaves divided into three leaflets, and white or red flowers in summer. Clover is useful because it's excellent at taking nitrogen from the air. Nitrogen is an element essential to all plants, and it makes up about two-thirds of Earth's air. Clover roots absorb large amounts of it from air pockets in the soil and turn it into a form that the clover can use. When the clover dies, or a farmer plows it into the ground, the nitrogen in the plant is added to the soil. This leaves the soil more fertile, which benefits other plants.

Clover's relatives, including peas and beans, also absorb nitrogen. A long time ago, farmers realized that these plants were natural fertilizers. They began to rotate their crops by planting a different one in the same field every year. Every few years, they would sow clover, peas, or beans to increase the soil's fertility and help it recover. Today, artificial fertilizers may be used instead, but these take a lot of energy to make and can harm the environment.

White clover
(Trifolium repens)
People have taken clover all over the world because it is so important to farming. White clover's wild home is Europe and western Asia.

Fixing nitrogen
Clover roots are covered in tiny lumps that are full of bacteria. These tiny organisms absorb nitrogen and convert it to a form that helps the clover grow, in a process called nitrogen fixing. When the clover dies, its nitrogen goes into the soil.

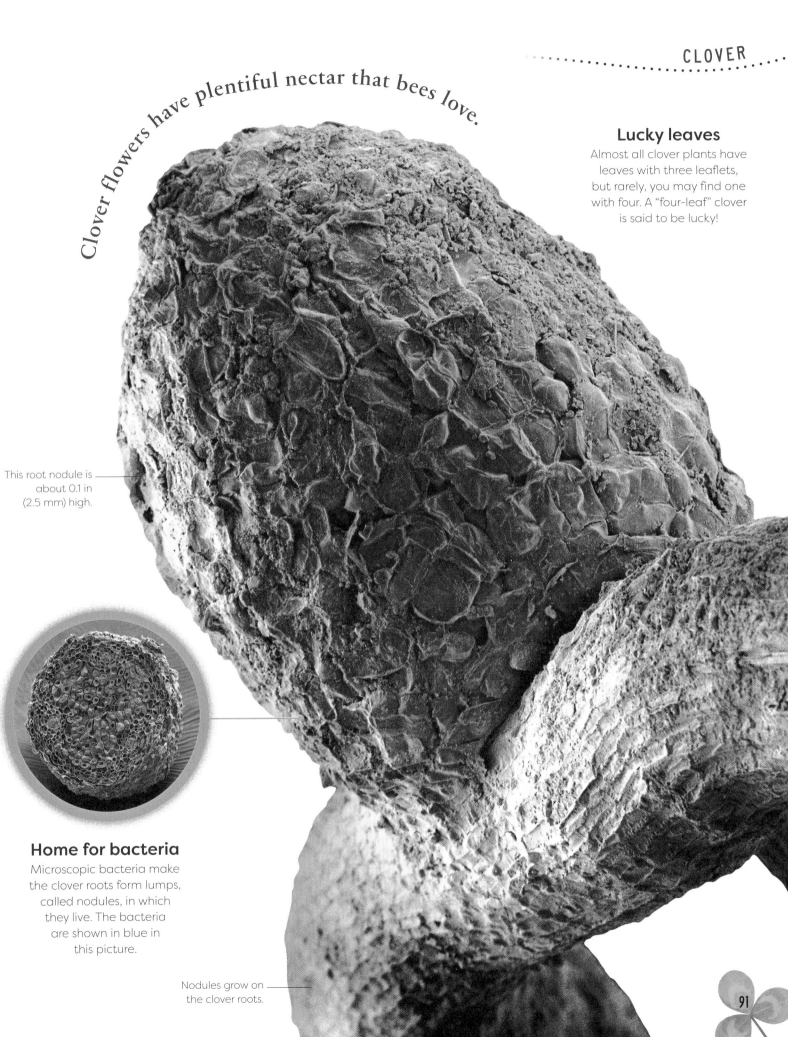

Clover flowers have plentiful nectar that bees love.

Lucky leaves

Almost all clover plants have leaves with three leaflets, but rarely, you may find one with four. A "four-leaf" clover is said to be lucky!

This root nodule is about 0.1 in (2.5 mm) high.

Home for bacteria

Microscopic bacteria make the clover roots form lumps, called nodules, in which they live. The bacteria are shown in blue in this picture.

Nodules grow on the clover roots.

91

Buttress roots

The kapok's supporting roots are called buttress roots. They reach out along the forest floor to hold up the trunk and keep it stable.

Top of the forest

Kapoks emerge above the rain forest canopy. Their leaves are not crowded by other trees, so they are bathed in sunlight and can carry out as much photosynthesis as possible. Forest giants that grow in this way are known as emergent trees.

Damp hollows between the roots shelter many small animals, such as the ratlike agouti.

Fluffy seeds

Kapok seeds are covered in white fluff, like cotton, and give the tree its other name of silk-cotton tree. The fibers can be used to make clothes.

Kapok

The giant kapok tree has huge roots above ground to prop up its trunk.

Birds and monkeys perching in the top of a kapok tree have a wonderful view of the surrounding forest. This is a tree that soars high above the others, like a giraffe among a herd of zebras. It can grow up to 230 ft (70 m) high! There is a problem with being so tall, though. The soil in tropical rain forests, where the kapok lives, is thin and lacks nutrients. Over millions of years, most of the minerals have been washed away, and the rain forest is so hot and wet that leaves soon rot when they fall, rather than adding their nutrients to the soil. This means the kapok's roots do not go very deep. To stop itself from falling over, some of its roots grow into thick supports that extend from its trunk and stretch over the ground like spread fingers.

The kapok is a sacred tree for many peoples in Central and South America. In Maya legend, it is the tree of life—with roots reaching the underworld, its trunk supporting the human world, and its highest branches in heaven.

Kapok

(Ceiba pentandra)
The kapok is one of the tallest trees in Central and South America. It has also naturally spread to western Africa. High up on its trunk and branches, it has sharp spines.

93

Living root bridge

The Khasi people of northeastern India make living
bridges across deep river valleys. They place supports
from one riverbank to the other, so that fig trees can
grow their woody roots along them. Over many years,
the roots thicken and tangle around each other
to create a strong structure.

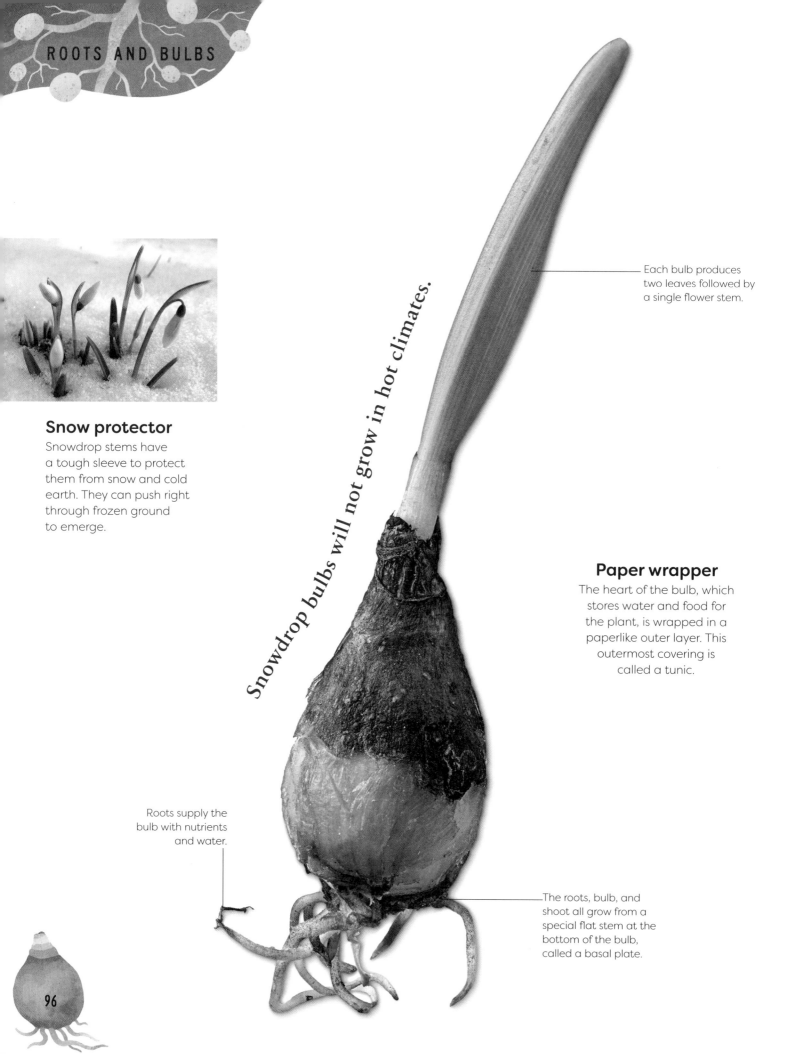

Each bulb produces two leaves followed by a single flower stem.

Snowdrop bulbs will not grow in hot climates.

Snow protector

Snowdrop stems have a tough sleeve to protect them from snow and cold earth. They can push right through frozen ground to emerge.

Paper wrapper

The heart of the bulb, which stores water and food for the plant, is wrapped in a paperlike outer layer. This outermost covering is called a tunic.

Roots supply the bulb with nutrients and water.

The roots, bulb, and shoot all grow from a special flat stem at the bottom of the bulb, called a basal plate.

Snowdrop

Snowdrops grow from bulbs that wait in the soil until winter to flower.

The droopy flowers of snowdrops poke above ground in the middle of winter. Their bell-like petals are white as snow, often with delicate pale green patterns. You might think these flowers look fragile. In fact, snowdrops are tough little plants. They burst into bloom even when the soil has frozen hard and is buried under snow. In Europe and North America, they are much-loved garden plants, but they only grow well where winters are cool. It may seem strange to flower in the coldest and darkest part of the year! However, snowdrops use the energy stored underground in their bulbs during earlier growing seasons to make sure they are one of the first plants in the year to emerge. Their grape-sized bulbs contain everything they need to produce leaves and flowers.

Snowdrops have many old names, including "snow-piercers" and "dingle-dangles." People always looked forward to seeing these cheerful flowers and believed that they were a hopeful sign for the year ahead. The flowers are a symbol of the Christian festival of Candlemas, which is celebrated on February 2.

Common snowdrop
(Galanthus nivalis)
People first cultivated snowdrop bulbs several hundred years ago. The plants prefer to live in the shade of trees and are originally from Europe's woodlands.

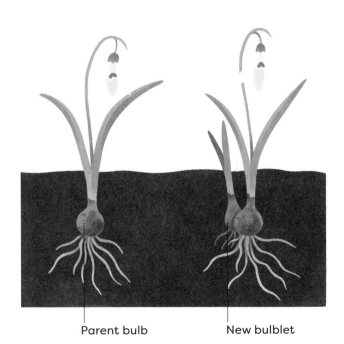

Parent bulb   New bulblet

Baby bulblets
As well as spreading by seeds, snowdrops can spread directly from their bulbs. Older snowdrop bulbs develop buds, called bulblets, around the outside. The bulblets grow using energy from the parent bulb and send out roots of their own, then split off to form new plants.

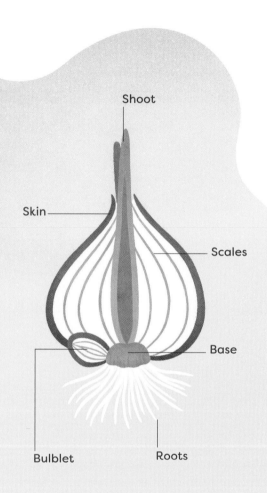

Shoot

Skin

Scales

Base

Bulblet   Roots

Inside a bulb

The base of a bulb grows roots and many
layers of fleshy leaves, called scales, where
it stores food and water. When conditions
are right, the bulb sends up green leaves.
Many bulbs are poisonous to eat.

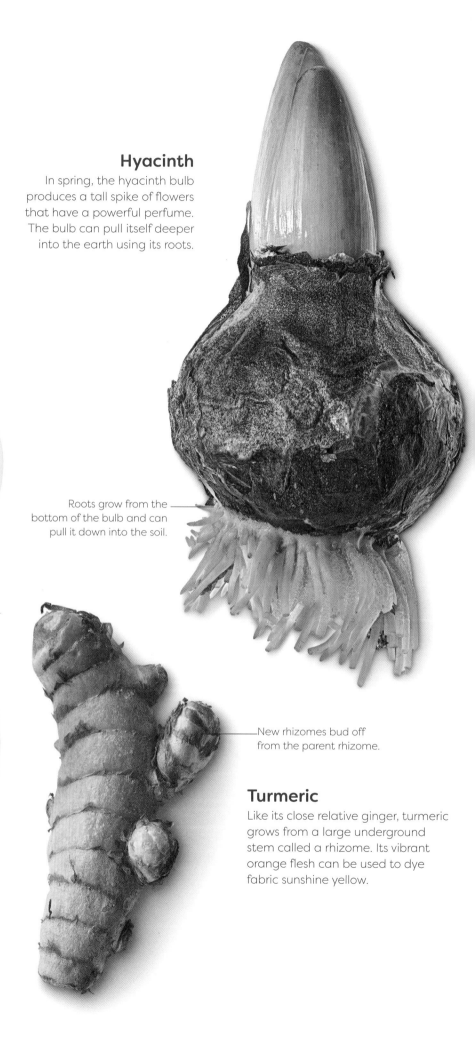

Hyacinth

In spring, the hyacinth bulb
produces a tall spike of flowers
that have a powerful perfume.
The bulb can pull itself deeper
into the earth using its roots.

Roots grow from the
bottom of the bulb and can
pull it down into the soil.

New rhizomes bud off
from the parent rhizome.

Turmeric

Like its close relative ginger, turmeric
grows from a large underground
stem called a rhizome. Its vibrant
orange flesh can be used to dye
fabric sunshine yellow.

Underground stores

When it is too cold, hot, or dry for plants to grow, many survive by dying back above ground and living off the supplies of food and water they have built up in underground stores. They pack nutrients inside swollen roots or stems, or in round structures called bulbs.

Lily

In the wild in Asia and Europe, lilies spend the winter safe underground as bulbs. We grow them for their stunning sweet-scented flowers, which emerge in summer.

Crown fritillary

This huge bulb is as big as an orange and has a hole on top. Its flowers have an unusual foxlike smell, which people claim scares off rats and mice.

Onion

Onions come from southwestern Asia, but are grown worldwide for their tasty bulbs. When we cut into their flesh, it releases chemicals that make us cry.

Oca

Oca plants have fat underground stems, known as tubers, which look like knobbly toes. They were one of the first vegetables planted by people and come in many colors.

Sweet potato

The sweet potato is from tropical parts of South America. It isn't related to other types of potato, but its swollen roots are used in a similar way—although it tastes sweeter.

Carrot

Most people don't realize that carrots are actually large roots. Originally, carrots had white flesh and were inedible, but breeding led to today's orange vegetables.

Tulip patterns are common in Islamic art.

Bulbs are planted with the pointed end at the top.

Semper Augustus

The rarest and most valuable tulip in history was a variety called Semper Augustus. In 1636, one of its bulbs cost more than a large house!

Hybrid tulips

New varieties of tulips are called hybrid tulips. To make them, plant breeders choose two kinds of tulips and brush pollen from one onto the other, then grow the seeds created.

A tulip bulb's outer skin is brown and papery.

Tulip

Tulips are among the world's most famous flowers. People have planted their bulbs for centuries.

Few flowers have excited and dazzled people as much as tulips. They are named after the Persian word for "turban" because of the way their beautiful petals wrap around each other. Wild tulips are mostly reddish, yellow, or pink. They grow back each year from a fleshy bulb that spends winter resting in the cold soil, and flower in spring. Through careful breeding, over 30,000 varieties exist today that come in all the colors of the rainbow!

During the early 1600s, tulips became very fashionable in the Netherlands. The craze was known as tulipomania. Before long, people were paying enormous sums of money to get their hands on the rarest bulbs. Some of the most unusually patterned tulips were actually infected with a virus that made their petals streaked, but this wasn't understood at the time. To this day, the Netherlands is still the main grower of tulips. From the air, its tulip fields are blocks of brilliant color, as if the earth itself has been painted.

Tulip
(Tulipa)
Garden tulips have many petal shapes, colors, and patterns. Their ancestors grow wild in northern and central Asia, and eastern Europe.

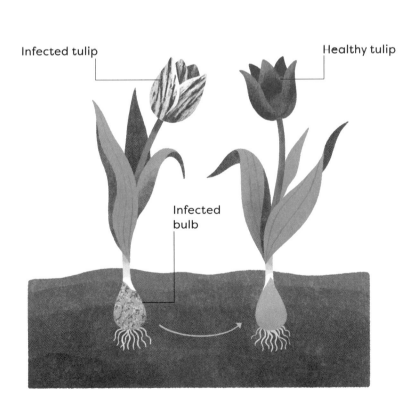

Infected tulip

Healthy tulip

Infected bulb

Infected bulb

Tulip petals sometimes have streaks of other colors. In the past, these marks were caused by a virus that infected the bulb. If the infection spread to other bulbs, those tulips also often became streaky. Today, multicolored petals have been bred on purpose.

CHAPTER 4

Flowers

Once, there were no flowers on Earth. The first blooms probably appeared more than 130 million years ago. Today, they come in a spectacular variety of forms—some tiny, others giant—and fill the world with fabulous colors and scents. A few reek of things that are much less pleasant! But whatever they look or smell like, flowers have a vital role to play. They are how most plants reproduce.

Seagrass

This is the only plant that erupts into flower on the ocean floor.

Parts of the seabed are as green as any lawn. These underwater fields lie in shallow water just offshore, often where rivers flow into the sea. If you dove down for a closer look, you would see long, green ribbons swirling in the current. At first, you might think you're looking at seaweed, which is a kind of algae, but this is seagrass, a flowering plant. Unlike seaweed, it has leaves, roots, flowers, seeds, and fruits. The unusual male and female flowers of tape seagrass grow on different stems. The ocean waves carry the male flowers, and their pollen, to the floating female ones.

Seagrass meadows are a home for shrimps and crabs, and the leaves are nibbled by turtles and fish. There is even a shark, called the bonnethead, that eats seagrass! Dugongs and manatees, which are large, slow-swimming mammals, graze the meadows like herds of cows. As it grows, seagrass takes large amounts of carbon from the sea and stores it in its leaves and roots. This stops the carbon from entering the air as carbon dioxide, which traps heat and makes our planet warm up. In this way, seagrass helps fight climate change.

Tape seagrass
(*Enhalus acoroides*)
Seagrasses look like grass, but they belongs to different families of plants. The largest meadows of seagrass are in bays and river mouths. This species grows in warm parts of the Indian and Pacific Oceans.

Seagrass ecosystem
Seagrass shapes and protects an ocean ecosystem. Its roots hold onto mud and sand, and its leaves slow ocean currents, which prevents the seabed from washing away. Its leaves also shelter small animals and are food for species such as manatees.

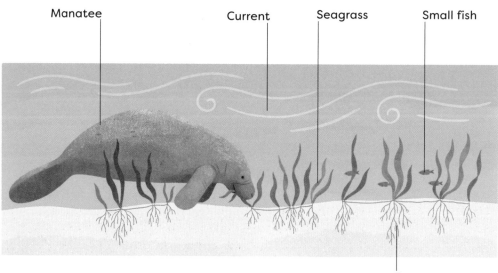

Manatee   Current   Seagrass   Small fish

Roots

Seagrasses produce fruits
that bob along on the
waves before sinking
to the seafloor.

Tape seagrass
flowers float on the
surface of the ocean.

The stigma of the
female flower is large,
so that it can catch
floating male flowers.

Flowering underwater

Pollen from male seagrass
flowers drifts through the
ocean or at the surface until
it arrives at female seagrass
flowers and pollinates them.

Seagrass only grows
in shallow water
because it needs
plenty of sunlight.

Kelp forest

Kelp is a large seaweed that
grows on the seabed and
creates thick forests. Some
can be 150 ft (45 m) tall!

Pearlwort flowers are tiny, yellow stars.

Hairy grass

Antarctic hair grass is the only other flowering plant in Antarctica. It looks shaggy—like untidy hair that needs brushing!

The leaves form a springy cushion, similar to moss.

Pearlwort hugs the ground and grows just 2 in (5 cm) high.

Winter snow

Antarctic pearlwort can survive very low temperatures and being buried under snow for many months.

Antarctic pearlwort

Pearlwort flowers bring a splash of color to one of the harshest environments on Earth.

Long ago, Antarctica was warm and mostly forest. Millions of years later, it is a world of snow and ice, where the winds are ferocious and temperatures dive below –40°F (–40°C). This land has no trees or bushes but, even here, there are patches of green. In sheltered places you can find moss and two flowering plants—one is Antarctic pearlwort. Its biggest challenge is the Antarctic winter, the longest and coldest on Earth. From April to September, the sun never rises and the continent is plunged into darkness. Without sunlight, photosynthesis is not possible, and for six months the pearlwort rests. It does all its growing in summer, when the frozen ground thaws. Melting ice and snow provide it with freshwater. However, the pearlwort has another problem. What will pollinate its flowers? The only insects in Antarctica are tiny midges—and they can't fly, which means they are unable to do it. No seabirds that visit Antarctica can pollinate plants, and there are no other land animals. The solution? The pearlwort pollinates itself.

Antarctic pearlwort
(Colobanthus quitensis)
This plant lives in sheltered parts of Antarctica, but is spreading to new areas because climate change is making summers there warmer.

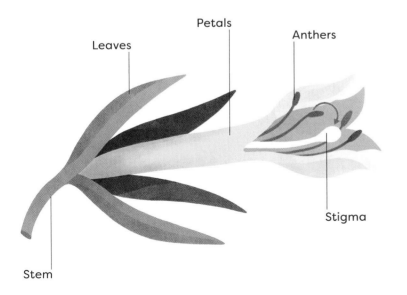

Leaves

Petals

Anthers

Stigma

Stem

Self-pollination

Antarctic pearlwort carries out self-pollination. This occurs when pollen from the anthers falls onto the stigma of the same flower, or reaches another flower on the same plant. Most plants try to avoid self-pollination because it means their offspring are very similar to them and may be less adaptable to changes in the environment.

Foxglove

The foxglove has spectacular flowers and is the source of a life-saving medicine.

According to legend, the foxglove is home to fairies. People once believed that the patterns on its flowers were their handprints! Then, in the 1780s, an English doctor made an important discovery. He found that chemicals in foxgloves have a strong effect on the human heart. They are the main ingredients of digitalis, a medicine used to treat heart failure. However, the same chemicals can also be fatal. This means the flowers, seeds, leaves, and every other part of foxgloves are poisonous, so they should never be eaten.

Foxgloves produce their tall spikes of flowers in summer. Often they grow in clearings in woods, where a gap in the trees lets in more sunlight. When trees are felled or blown down in storms, it creates new clearings and foxgloves are some of the first plants to appear. How are they so quick? It's because they spread huge quantities of seeds after flowering, so the woodland soil is full of foxglove seeds, all waiting for the chance to grow. A single flowering stem can release a million seeds.

Purple foxglove
(Digitalis purpurea)
The foxglove is one of Europe's prettiest wildflowers. It lives in woods, beside roads and railroads, and on waste ground.

Two-year life cycle

Foxglove plants are biennials and live for just two years. They take a year to grow roots and leaves and do not bloom until the following summer. Once a foxglove's flowers have been pollinated, they develop seeds and the plant dies. The dry flowers fall off, which scatters the seeds.

Year 1:
Leaves

Year 2:
Flowers

Year 2:
Seedheads

The flower buds at the top of the stem are the last to open.

Bees adore the sweet nectar of foxglove flowers.

Wild foxgloves are usually purple, which is one of the colors bees can see most clearly.

Spotty pattern

The spots and lines inside the flowers are called nectar guides, as they point bees in the direction of the sweet nectar.

Hard to reach

Only insects with a long tongue can reach the nectar at the bottom of the funnel-like flowers. Their main pollinators are bumblebees.

Each foxglove has one flowering stem. All of its leaves are at the base.

109

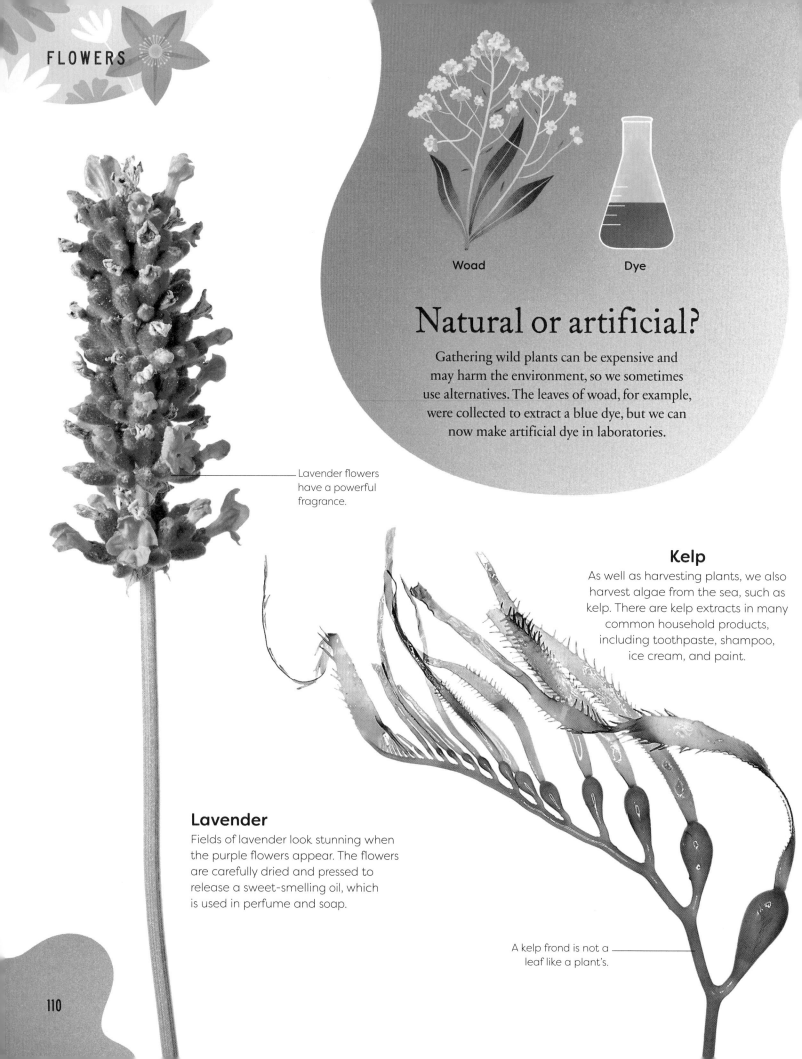

Woad

Dye

Natural or artificial?

Gathering wild plants can be expensive and may harm the environment, so we sometimes use alternatives. The leaves of woad, for example, were collected to extract a blue dye, but we can now make artificial dye in laboratories.

Lavender flowers have a powerful fragrance.

Kelp

As well as harvesting plants, we also harvest algae from the sea, such as kelp. There are kelp extracts in many common household products, including toothpaste, shampoo, ice cream, and paint.

Lavender

Fields of lavender look stunning when the purple flowers appear. The flowers are carefully dried and pressed to release a sweet-smelling oil, which is used in perfume and soap.

A kelp frond is not a leaf like a plant's.

Plant products

Early humans had hundreds of uses for plants. They learned where to find each species and how to harvest it, taking only what they needed. This plant knowledge has been passed on, and to this day, plants are still essential to every part of our lives.

Cotton

The cotton plant is grown for its large, fluffy seedpods, from which we obtain white fibers. The fibers are spun into threads to make cotton cloth, which is both soft and strong.

Henna

Leaves of the henna plant are made into a paste to make a reddish-brown dye. Artists draw patterns on people's skin with it—often for traditional Muslim and Hindu weddings.

Papyrus

Papyrus is a grasslike plant called a sedge, found on riverbanks and in marshes. In ancient Egypt, its stalks were cut and arranged in layers, then pressed, to make thick sheets of paper.

Aloe vera

This plant is from southwestern Asia but is now grown in many warm countries. Its thick leaves contain a see-through gel that may soothe sunburn and other skin conditions.

Sandalwood

The inner part, or heartwood, of sandalwood trees can be turned into powder or oil with a pleasant perfume. Hindus mark their forehead with a paste that includes sandalwood to show their faith.

Willow

In the bark of willow trees is a chemical called salicin. This is gathered and concentrated to make aspirin, one of the most common medicines for treating pain and fevers.

Strong seeds

Once the seeds are ripe, they are released into the water and float away. These tough capsules have been able to sprout after more than 1,000 years!

The lotus effect

Lotus leaves have tiny bumps that stop rain and dirt from sticking. Water droplets slide off their surface, so the leaves stay clean and shiny.

Several rings of curled pink petals form a rosette.

The seeds are made in a yellow cone at the center of the flower.

Lotus pollen is made by the male anthers, which surround the central cone.

Hindu gods are often pictured sitting on lotus flowers.

Lotus

This wetland flower plays a major part in the art and culture of Asia.

At certain times of the year, lakes and ponds in Asia suddenly turn pink. At first, there is nothing to be seen except for a sea of round leaves sticking up from the water. Soon, though, taller stalks bearing buds pop up, and the blooms all open together. For just a few days, the water is covered with thousands of lotus flowers, each as big as a dinner plate. Their bright color and strong scent attract pollinating beetles. The flowers are attached to the mud at the bottom of the water by a strong stem that acts like a ship's anchor. Many animals live among the masses of lotus plants. Turtles, frogs, and fish hide under the floating leaves, and water birds walk across them, using them as stepping stones.

The lotus flower inspires artists and writers with its beauty. In much of Asia, it stands for purity, and it is sacred to Hindus, Sikhs, and Buddhists. In India and Vietnam, it is the national flower. Lotus plants are also popular as food. The young leaves and crunchy, rootlike rhizomes are served as vegetables, and the seeds are toasted as a snack.

Lotus
(Nelumbo nucifera)
The lotus grows in shallow water in warm parts of southern and eastern Asia, from India all the way to Japan.

Beetles fly in

Flower closes

Beetles are covered in pollen

Beetle prisoners
Lotus flowers heat up and release perfume to tempt beetles to them, then close overnight to trap the insects inside! Next morning, the flowers open to release the beetles, now covered in pollen. When the beetles visit another lotus flower, they pollinate it with the pollen.

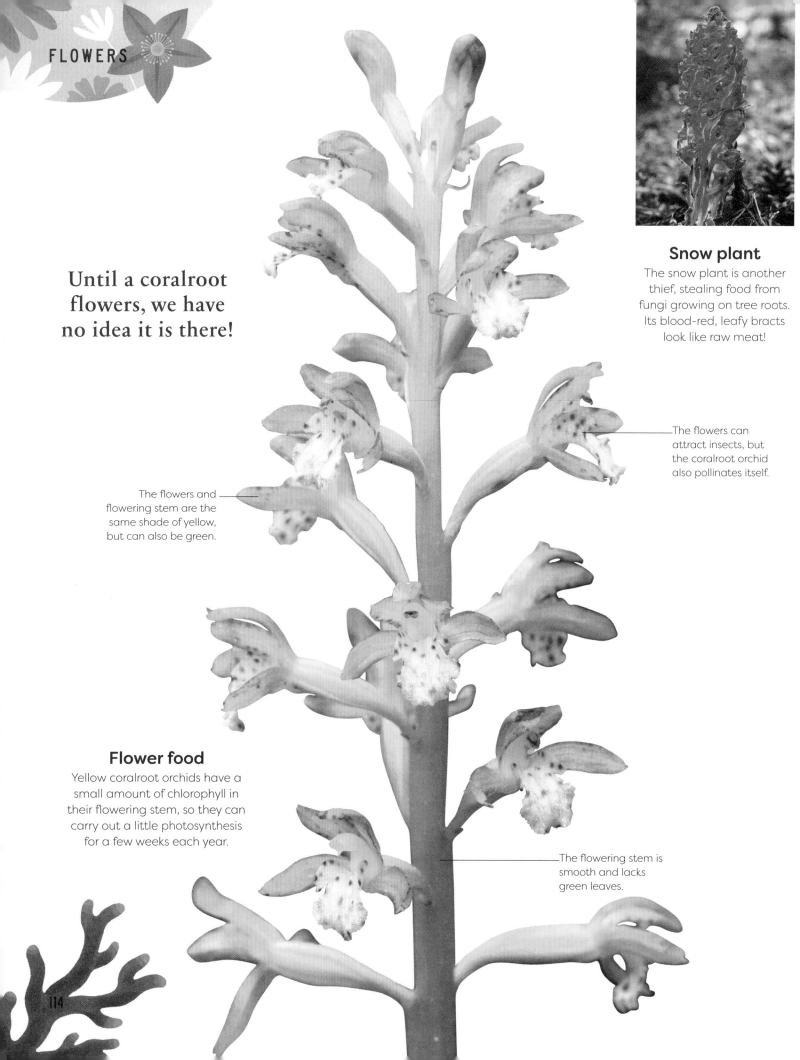

Until a coralroot flowers, we have no idea it is there!

Snow plant

The snow plant is another thief, stealing food from fungi growing on tree roots. Its blood-red, leafy bracts look like raw meat!

The flowers can attract insects, but the coralroot orchid also pollinates itself.

The flowers and flowering stem are the same shade of yellow, but can also be green.

Flower food

Yellow coralroot orchids have a small amount of chlorophyll in their flowering stem, so they can carry out a little photosynthesis for a few weeks each year.

The flowering stem is smooth and lacks green leaves.

Coralroot orchid

The flowers are all we see of these strange and sneaky plants that lurk in the soil.

Plants usually make their own food using energy from sunlight, but a few are vampires. They attack the stems or roots of other plants and suck out water, nutrients, and sugar. Coralroot orchids are one of these; however, their victims are not plants. They steal from networks of fungi living in the soil. For around 11 months of the year, they stay hidden below ground, feeding off the fungi. Then, in midsummer, they produce long stems of flowers, which often emerge under trees. The flowers are quite small and don't appear every year, but if you do spot one, you will have found one of the world's sneakiest plants.

Several weeks later, after they have produced seeds, the flowers shrivel and the coralroot orchids return to their odd underground life. Plants that steal what they need are known as parasites. Some cannot make any food of their own, which means they are totally dependent on their host. If it dies, they die. Others, including coralroot orchids, are able to make a little food and steal the rest.

Yellow coralroot
(Corallorhiza trifida)
Coralroot orchids are named for their stubby roots, which look like coral. Yellow coralroot lives in forests in Asia, Europe, and North America.

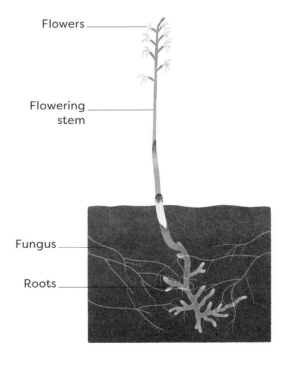

Flowers

Flowering stem

Fungus

Roots

Roots that steal
Coralroot orchids have thick, lumpy roots that provide a snug home for soil fungi. The orchids take some water, nutrients, and sugars from the fungi they live with, but never enough to harm or kill them.

115

Corpse flower

The stinking bloom that this plant produces is the largest flower on Earth.

Among the fallen leaves in a tropical rain forest, a monster is stirring. At first, there is little to see. A shoot pushes up through the soil and starts to fatten. Very slowly, it swells into what seems to be a leathery cabbage. Eventually, the corpse flower shows itself. Its bud bursts open and reveals a gigantic bloom over 3 ft (1 m) wide. The flower looks and smells like a dead animal. Soon it is covered in flies and beetles, which think they have found a tasty meal of rotting meat. They crawl into the mouthlike opening at the heart of the flower, and leave with sticky pollen all over them. The corpse flower doesn't have other plant parts, and it is unable to carry out photosynthesis. It is a parasite, which seizes food and supplies from others. Its victims are vines climbing up rain forest trees. The corpse flower actually lives inside the vines, where it grows thousands of threads, like a fungus, that snatch everything it needs until it is ready to produce its supersized flower.

Corpse flower
(*Rafflesia arnoldii*)
Corpse flowers live only in the rain forests of southeastern Asia. They are endangered, so very hard to find.

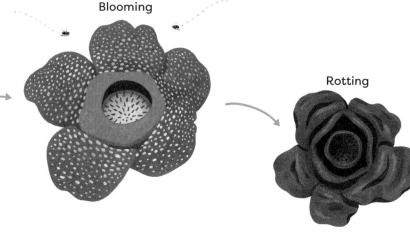

Blooming

Opening

Rotting

Bud

Brief bloom
The corpse flower's bud grows slowly—it takes one or two years until, finally, it unfolds its massive petals. The smelly flower lasts for only a few days before it begins to rot. Then it rapidly collapses in a soggy black heap.

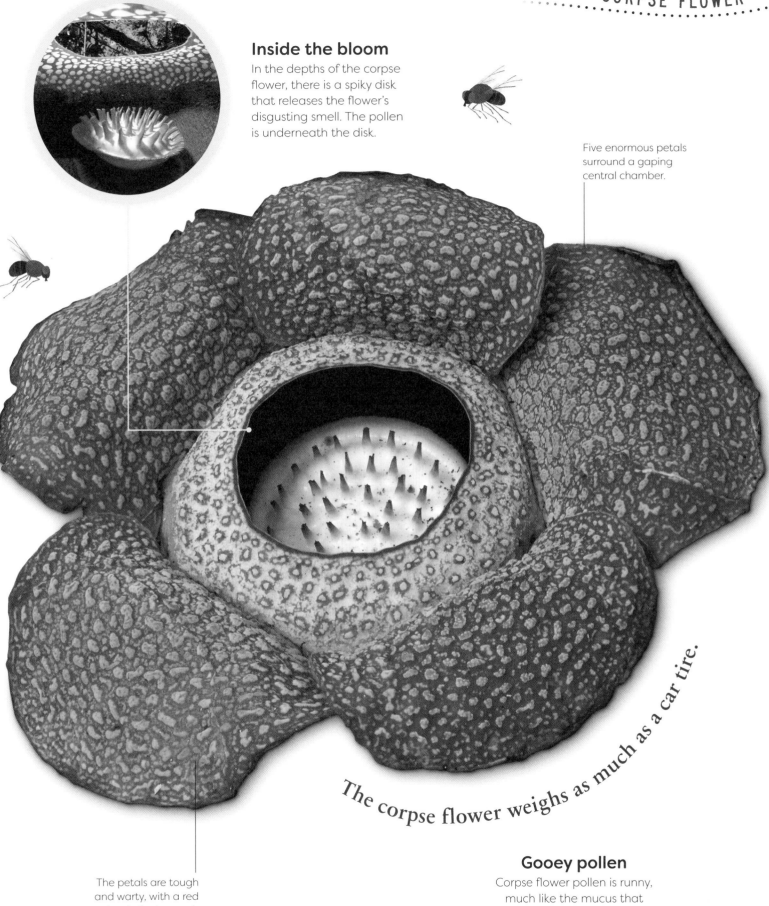

Inside the bloom

In the depths of the corpse flower, there is a spiky disk that releases the flower's disgusting smell. The pollen is underneath the disk.

Five enormous petals surround a gaping central chamber.

The petals are tough and warty, with a red color similar to meat.

The corpse flower weighs as much as a car tire.

Gooey pollen

Corpse flower pollen is runny, much like the mucus that comes out of your nose! Insects that enter the flower are soon coated in slimy goo.

117

Night pollination

The saguaro cactus opens its flowers after sunset. The flowers are white, so they shine in the light of the Moon, and fill the desert air with a scent like ripe melons. This attracts long-nosed bats, which end up with pollen all over their furry faces as they lap up the flower's nectar. The bats carry the pollen between flowers, pollinating them.

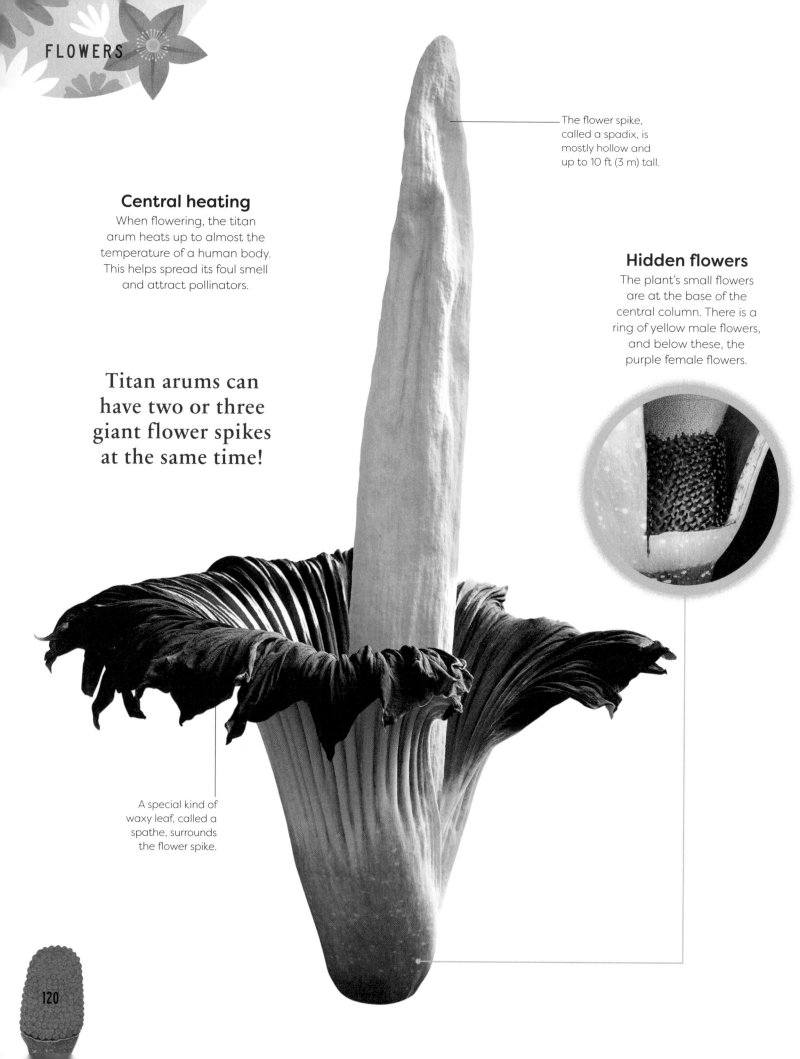

The flower spike, called a spadix, is mostly hollow and up to 10 ft (3 m) tall.

Central heating
When flowering, the titan arum heats up to almost the temperature of a human body. This helps spread its foul smell and attract pollinators.

Hidden flowers
The plant's small flowers are at the base of the central column. There is a ring of yellow male flowers, and below these, the purple female flowers.

Titan arums can have two or three giant flower spikes at the same time!

A special kind of waxy leaf, called a spathe, surrounds the flower spike.

Titan arum

The titan arum sends up an immense flower spike, which is extremely smelly, but lasts just for one day.

The titan arum is a star attraction at botanic gardens, which are like plant zoos. It is not easy to grow in a greenhouse, however, and may take 10 years to flower. When the plant finally blooms, crowds of people flock to see it. The colossal yellow flower spike is taller than any person. This is not a single flower, though. The petal-like, crimson wrapper hides a collection of many small flowers at the bottom of the spike. Visitors can smell the spike long before they set eyes on it. It gives off a vile stink—made by the chemicals found in rotting fish, sweaty socks, poo, and moldy cheese! The nasty smell gives the titan arum its other name of "corpse plant." Flies and beetles arrive in search of a dead animal, but they have been tricked—when they crawl in, there is no meat to be found. Instead, the plant uses the insects to pollinate its flowers. In the wild, the titan arum is very rare and under threat because its rain forest home is being cut down and cleared.

Titan arum
(*Amorphophallus titanum*)
Wild titan arums live only on Sumatra, an island in Indonesia. Most of the time they appear as a single, huge, Y-shaped leaf.

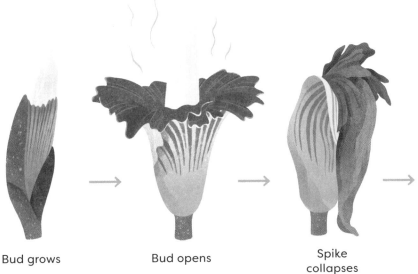

Bud grows → Bud opens → Spike collapses →  Fruits appear

Rapid growth

A titan arum stores energy in its underground stem for years before it produces a bud. The bud grows fast for several weeks, then one afternoon, the flower spike opens. It becomes warmer and smellier overnight, but wilts the next day. The fertilized flowers develop into a mass of little red fruits.

121

Wolfsbane

Wolfsbane flowers are beautiful but deadly. In fact, every part of this plant is highly toxic.

People have feared this plant for thousands of years. In summertime, its blue or pale purple flowers look handsome, yet should be left well alone—they contain poison. The poison is a chemical called aconitine, and it is found throughout the whole plant, including in its pollen, leaves, stems, and roots. Just a small amount of aconitine will cause severe sickness or sometimes death. The ancient Greeks knew all about wolfsbane, and smeared it onto their arrows and spears to hunt wolves and other dangerous animals. The ancient Romans used it to kill their enemies. In stories, wolfsbane could frighten away legendary werewolves, which is how the plant earned its name.

Wolfsbane is one of many plants that are poisonous to humans. The planet actually has more toxic species than edible ones! Poison is one of many defenses that plants use to avoid being eaten. Plants may be inedible to animals that would damage them, but not to those who might pollinate them or help spread their seeds. Many birds can eat berries that would harm mammals, but spread the seeds in their droppings.

Wolfsbane
(Aconitum napellus)
Wolfsbane lives in Europe, and has a relative in North America that is also toxic. Gardeners grow both species but handle them with gloves.

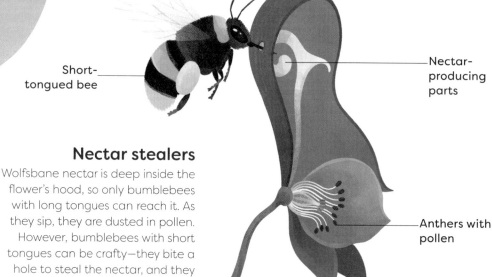

Short-tongued bee

Nectar-producing parts

Anthers with pollen

Nectar stealers

Wolfsbane nectar is deep inside the flower's hood, so only bumblebees with long tongues can reach it. As they sip, they are dusted in pollen. However, bumblebees with short tongues can be crafty—they bite a hole to steal the nectar, and they don't pollinate the flower.

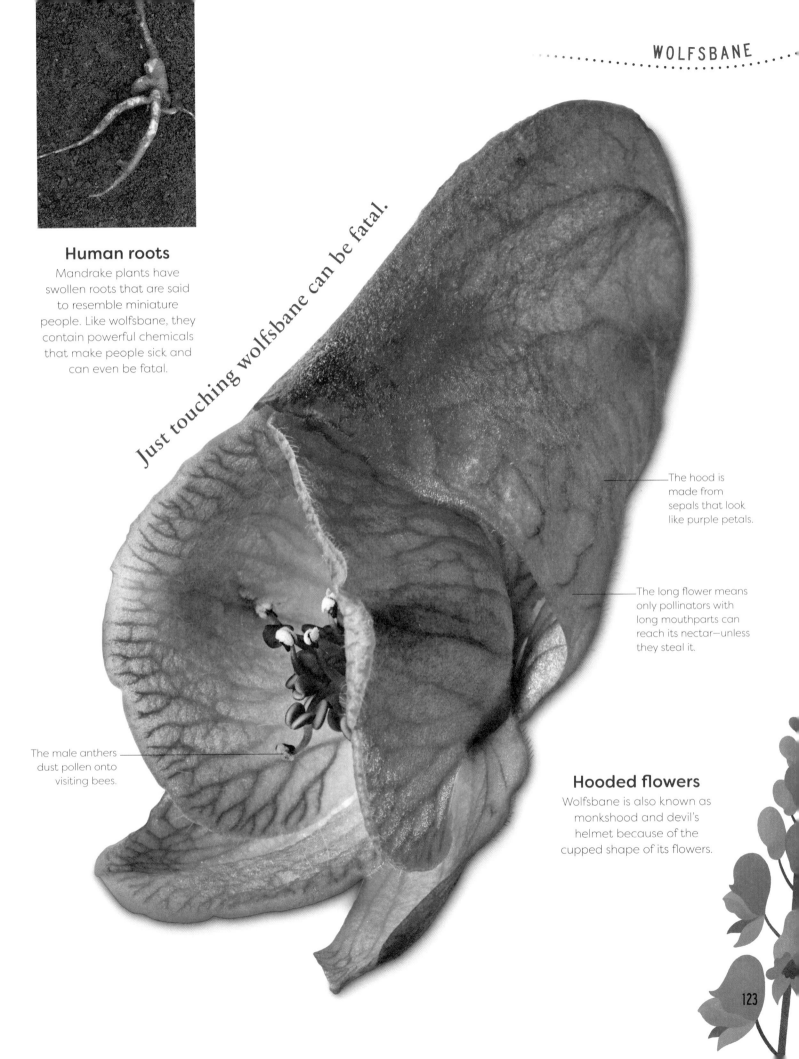

Human roots

Mandrake plants have swollen roots that are said to resemble miniature people. Like wolfsbane, they contain powerful chemicals that make people sick and can even be fatal.

Just touching wolfsbane can be fatal.

The hood is made from sepals that look like purple petals.

The long flower means only pollinators with long mouthparts can reach its nectar—unless they steal it.

The male anthers dust pollen onto visiting bees.

Hooded flowers

Wolfsbane is also known as monkshood and devil's helmet because of the cupped shape of its flowers.

123

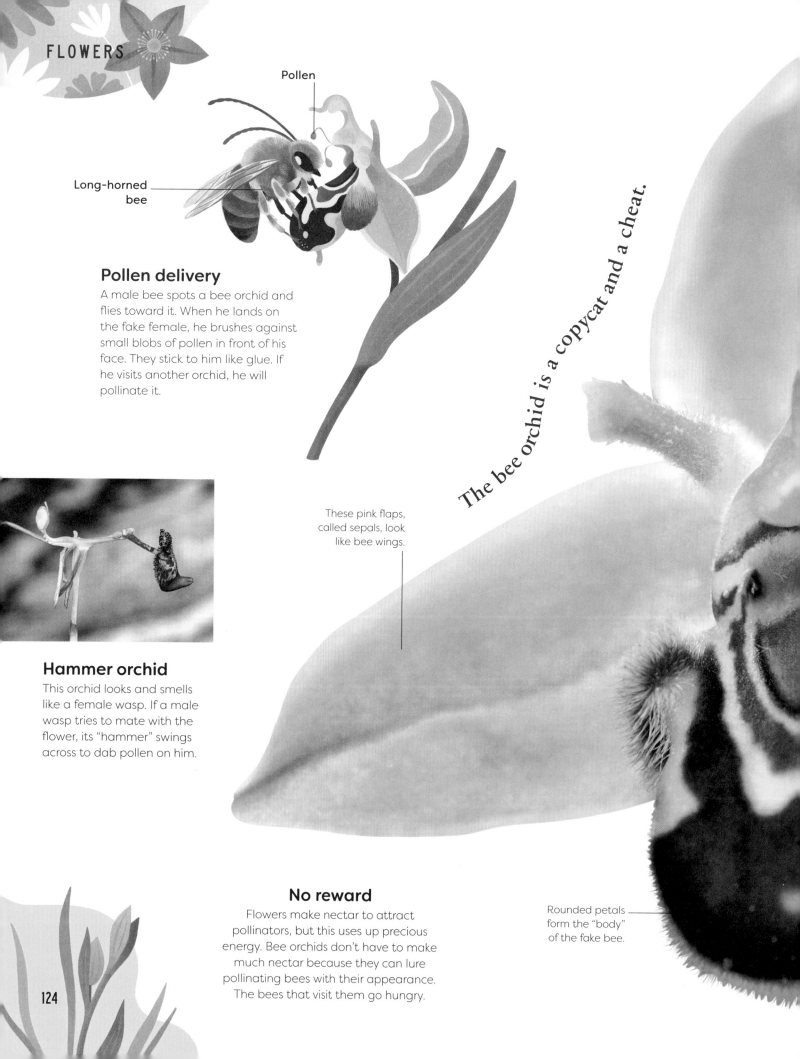

Pollen

Long-horned
bee

Pollen delivery

A male bee spots a bee orchid and flies toward it. When he lands on the fake female, he brushes against small blobs of pollen in front of his face. They stick to him like glue. If he visits another orchid, he will pollinate it.

Hammer orchid

This orchid looks and smells like a female wasp. If a male wasp tries to mate with the flower, its "hammer" swings across to dab pollen on him.

The bee orchid is a copycat and a cheat.

These pink flaps, called sepals, look like bee wings.

Rounded petals form the "body" of the fake bee.

No reward

Flowers make nectar to attract pollinators, but this uses up precious energy. Bee orchids don't have to make much nectar because they can lure pollinating bees with their appearance. The bees that visit them go hungry.

Bee orchid

The bee orchid does a good impression of a bee—a clever way to attract real bees.

Long, yellow structures look like antennae.

Orchids are the second largest family of flowering plants. There are nearly 30,000 species, many of which have dazzling flowers. Some offer a sugary gift of nectar to encourage insects to visit and pollinate them, just as other plants do. However, around a third of the world's orchids are not so honest. They trick insects into pollinating them and do not give anything in return. The bee orchid does exactly this to the long-horned bee. It imitates the female of this species by copying her shape, color, feel, and scent. When a male bee arrives to mate with what he believes is a suitable partner, the orchid's pollen is smeared on his body. The poor bee flies off to find another "bee" and, if he is tricked again, the pollen is transferred to that flower, pollinating it.

Many scientists have studied orchids and their relationship with bees and other insects. It seems incredible that these flowers can be so good at mimicking what insects look like, because they don't have eyes, so can't even see what they are copying!

Bee orchid
(Ophrys apifera)
This orchid is found in grassy places in Europe and northern Africa, often on roadsides or empty lots.

125

Copycat plants

Plants may lack eyes and a brain, but they are very good at copying other things, including different plants, animals, and fungi. They can mimic how those species look, smell, or feel. Often their disguise helps them attract pollinators, but it may also keep plant-eating insects away.

Passionflower

This vine has spots on its leaves that seem to be butterfly eggs. Real butterflies want fresh leaves to lay their eggs on, so ignore them, and the vine avoids leaf-eating caterpillars.

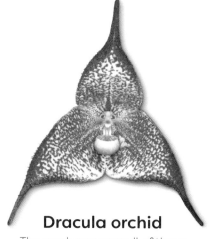

Dracula orchid

The mushroomy smell of these South American flowers drifts through the air. It attracts flies that feed on fungi, which become covered in pollen instead.

Red dead-nettle

The dead-nettle is harmless, but it has hairy, wavy-edged leaves that look like stinging nettles. This tricks hungry animals, which move elsewhere to find a safer meal!

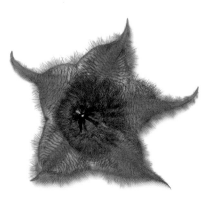

Starfish flower

This plant is one of many that copy the meaty appearance and smell of dead animals, or carrion. It is soon buzzing with flies, which pollinate its stinky flowers.

Pawpaw

The US's pawpaw tree has curious flowers that smell strongly of rotting fruit. When fruit flies arrive for a meal, they are fooled and end up pollinating the flowers instead.

Star orchid

This orchid mimics two other flowers that are full of nectar. But, unlike them, it has none. Any insects that visit the sneaky orchid will pollinate it but receive nothing in return.

Karoo rose

You have to search very hard to spot this plant because it matches the stones of its desert home. Grazing animals are also fooled, which is how the plant avoids being eaten.

The leaves are smooth, chunky, and stone-colored, just like pebbles.

Calypso orchid

The calypso orchid attracts bumblebees with fake pollen and nectar. The bees try to feed, with no success. Meanwhile, sticky blobs of the orchid's real pollen attach to them and they carry it away.

This flower is shaped like a slipper, with a yellow target for bees to land on.

Insect gardener

One grasslike plant tricks dung beetles into planting its seeds, which look and smell like balls of antelope poo! The beetles think they have found the perfect food for their grubs, so they roll the seeds away and bury them, only for them to sprout.

127

Hot pink

Flowers contain colorful pigments, which produce their bright shades. It is thought that the amount of each pigment in a hibiscus varies according to the temperature.

Hibiscus tea

This thirst-quenching drink is made from the dried flowers of several plants in the hibiscus family, including the Chinese hibiscus.

The cotton rose needs plenty of sunlight to flower.

The yellow center of the cotton rose contains its seed- and pollen-producing parts.

Green, leaflike sepals protect the flower bud.

The flowers are large enough to cover the palm of your hand.

128

Hibiscus

As if by magic, hibiscus flowers can change color in a few hours.

Some animals can change the color of their skin. Chameleons and octopuses are famous for the speed of their amazing transformations. But plants don't have skin, so changes in their color are usually slow. For example, the leaves of deciduous trees take several days or weeks to turn from green to red and gold in the fall. However, a few plants are able to change color faster. The cotton rose, which is a species of hibiscus, has large flowers that can go from white to pale pink to dark pink in a day! Other varieties of hibiscus become bright red or orange.

The spectacular color change of hibiscus flowers is probably caused by a rise in temperature. If the flowers are put in a refrigerator to keep cool, they stay the same color. The horse chestnut tree also has color-changing flowers, but bees cause their transformation. The flowers start white with lines of yellow spots, but once they have been pollinated, their yellow markings turn red. This shows bees that the blooms have stopped making nectar, so the insects don't waste time visiting flowers with red markings.

Cotton rose
(*Hibiscus mutabilis*)
Many species of hibiscus have fabulous flowers, including the cotton rose from China, which is now grown worldwide.

Morning

Afternoon

Evening

Color change
In the cool of morning, the cotton rose has white flowers. By the middle of the day, its flowers blush pink in the warmth of the Sun. In the afternoon, as the temperature continues to rise, the flowers turn a deeper shade of pink. The pink flowers soon fall off the plant.

Blue bloom

The Himalayan blue poppy matches the color of the sky on a fine summer day. True blue flowers like this are very rare in nature, because blue pigment is difficult for plants to make. Most "blue" flowers actually reflect light to create the illusion of the color. This also saves the plant energy because colorful pigments used to attract pollinators cost energy to make.

Japanese cherry

Cherry tree blossom is celebrated with picnics and parties across Japan and around the world.

Japanese cherry
(*Prunus serrulata*)
There are many types of cherry trees but this is one of the most famous. It grows all over Japan, and is also found in China and other parts of eastern Asia.

In Japan, one type of tree is more important than all the others. Cherry trees, called sakura in Japanese, are planted in all kinds of places. You can see them beside roads, in long avenues in parks, and in temple gardens. The reason people love these trees so much becomes clear in March and April, when their beautiful pink flowers appear. Huge crowds head outside to view the blossoms, an ancient tradition known as hanami. People stroll and meet friends, and enjoy meals underneath the canopy of pink petals. The celebrations continue at night, when the blossom is lit up with colorful lanterns. The tradition of hanami began 1,200 years ago. It involves the entire nation, from the Japanese emperor to schoolchildren, and attracts tourists from around the world. The celebration has also spread to other countries. The blossom has a short life, though. Before long, it drifts to the ground like a shower of confetti. Records are kept of each year's cherry blossom season. They show that the blossom appears earlier now, because spring is arriving earlier due to climate change.

Blossom forecasts
It is warmer in the south of Japan, so cherry trees flower there first, followed by trees farther north. As spring moves north, a great wave of blossom sweeps through the country. Blossom forecasts predict when it will arrive in each area.

Cherry blossom only lasts a week before it falls.

Inedible fruit

Later in the year, the cherry trees produce fruits. Don't be tempted to try any, however—they are bad to eat and taste nasty, not like the cherries sold in stores.

The anthers, which produce pollen, are dark pink.

Double blossom

Expert plant breeders have created cherry trees with different types of blossoms. Some varieties have "double flowers," with more petals than usual. These types don't normally produce fruits.

Blossom forms in early spring. The tree's leaves develop afterward.

133

Common laburnum

The laburnum develops huge sprays of yellow blossoms that cover it completely—one of this tree's other names is "golden rain." Beware: this tree is highly poisonous.

Plum blossom

Plum fruit

Bright yellow blossoms are produced in spring.

From blossom to fruit

When blossoms are pollinated, in each individual flower a fruit will grow and ripen in the sun. Certain blossom trees provide some of our tastiest edible fruits, including apples, cherries, peaches, and plums.

Tassels of purple blossoms hang down from the branches.

Chinese wisteria

Wisteria is a climbing plant from China that is covered in pale purple blossoms in summer. It is grown worldwide, usually on supporting wires fixed to houses and walls. All parts of it are toxic.

Blossom

Some trees and bushes produce spectacular displays of flowers that we call blossoms. The blossoms often cover the whole plant before fading. Colorful sprays or bunches of flowers give pollinators a welcome feast and make a cheerful sight in towns and cities around the world.

Horse chestnut

This tall tree from southeastern Europe is common in city parks. Its magnificent white blossoms appear in spring and later develop into spiky, green fruits—conkers.

Apple

In spring, apple trees produce masses of white or pink blossoms that bees love. The fruits develop in the pollinated blossoms, and are ripe in the fall.

Flame tree

You can see how this Australian tree got its name! It is often planted in streets and parks, and unlike most trees, drops all its leaves before bursting into bloom.

Frangipani

This blossom tree, which is from Mexico and Central America, is grown for its sweet scent. The blossom smells like roses, ripe bananas, or cinnamon.

Jacaranda

The jacaranda is a familiar tree in many tropical cities, but originally came from Argentina and Brazil. Its pinkish-blue blossoms emerge in spring, before the tree grows leaves.

Rhododendron

A favorite with gardeners, these bushes grow wild in China and other parts of Asia. There are hundreds of species, all producing stunning blossoms in many colors.

CHAPTER 5

Fruits and cones

When we think of fruits, we think first of the varieties we can find in stores. But these are just a small selection of the fruits produced by the world's flowering plants. There are thousands of different types! A few are edible, but most are not—although there are often animals that can eat them. A fruit is formed when a flower is fertilized. Some plants that don't have flowers produce cones instead.

The skin of citrus fruits looks spotty because it contains tiny blobs of oil that have a strong smell. The oil protects the fruit from germs.

Unusual leaves

Leaves of pomelo trees seem to be in pairs. However, the lower "leaf" is actually a flat part of the stem.

Pomelo trees bear fruit all year round.

Full of air

Pomelo pith is a kind of natural cushion. It is full of tiny pockets of air that protect the flesh and seeds inside.

Pomelo skin may be greenish-yellow or bright green.

Pomelo

Huge and juicy, the pomelo is an ancestor of the citrus fruit we love today.

The fruits we see in stores, and grow on our farms and in our gardens, were once very different. Over hundreds of years, their color and taste have been changed through careful breeding. Many have been bred to have thinner peel and fewer pips—or none at all. Amazingly, the most common fruits in the citrus family, including oranges, tangerines, grapefruits, lemons, and limes, all came from just three wild ancestors: the citron, the mandarin, and the pomelo.

Breeding fruit varieties takes lots of time and patience. First, you select two trees of the same species whose fruit you like best. Next, you brush pollen from the flowers of one tree onto the flowers of the second tree. Finally, you plant the seeds created to grow a new tree. If you repeat this process over and over, the fruit you produce slowly changes. The pomelo was bred over many generations to create the grapefruit. Closely related plant species can sometimes be bred to make completely new types of fruit—a tangelo, for example, is a cross between a pomelo and a tangerine.

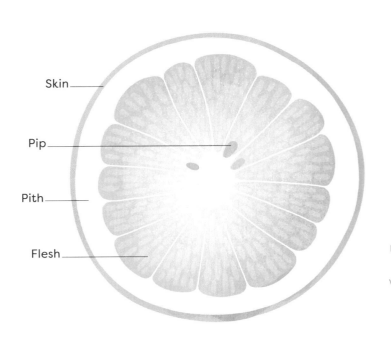

Pomelo
(*Citrus maxima*)
The pomelo is the world's largest citrus fruit, and can grow to be bigger than a soccer ball. It can still be found in the wild in southeastern Asia.

Skin

Pip

Pith

Flesh

Inside a citrus fruit

If you sliced a pomelo across the middle, this is what you would see. Under a layer of leathery skin, there is a white spongy cushion, called pith, which may be as thick as your thumb. The pith protects the segments of juicy flesh and the seeds, known as pips.

139

Strawberry

Sweet, red strawberries are a sugary treat. However, their "fruits" are not all they seem.

As they ripen in the warmth of the Sun, strawberries turn from green to red. The bold color change sends an urgent message: "I'm ready to eat." Many ripe fruits are red, because it's the color that shows up best against green leaves. Fruit-eaters, such as monkeys, have superb color vision to help them spot these sugary meals. Early humans also ate lots of wild fruit, so we too are alert to red things. This is why warning and stop signs are red. Other plants and animals use the color red to warn that they are poisonous.

In the wild, strawberry plants live in forests, where they spread across the ground using long stalks called runners. These take root to form new plants, which remain connected to the parent plant. Strawberries are easy to grow and are common in gardens and hanging baskets. Some farmers even grow them without soil—they stand the plants in trays of freshwater that has nutrients dissolved in it. Special lights that mimic the Sun mean they can be grown indoors.

Strawberry
(Fragaria x ananassa)
This is the strawberry plant we usually grow. It is a cross between two wild species, one from North America and the other from South America.

Ripe fruits

Unripe fruits

Flowers

Ripening strawberries
Strawberry plants produce fruit in an unusual way. Every flower contains many ovaries. When each ovary is pollinated, it makes a hard, yellow fruit attached to a fleshy stem. As they grow, the stems join together to create a single strawberry. At first, the flesh is green, but as it ripens, it turns red.

Strawberry plants belong to the rose family.

Sugar hit
Strawberries taste sweeter at room temperature. Our taste buds work differently when food is cold.

The seed inside each yellow fruit can grow into a whole new strawberry plant.

False fruit
The yellow dots on a strawberry are the real fruit, each with a seed inside. The fleshy part we eat is actually a juicy stem.

Useful fruits

Some fruits are bitter or hard, so only animals enjoy them. Others are poisonous. However, many are good for us, with flesh that's low in fat and rich in vitamins, minerals, and fiber. In some cases, the skin or peel of the fruits are also edible, and a few are grown just for their perfume.

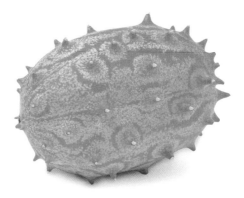

Kiwano

These spiny African fruits are also called horned melons. They are full of watery green jelly that tastes like cucumber, which people enjoy as a thirst-quenching treat.

Tomato

Tomatoes are not vegetables but fruits, because they develop from flowers and contain seeds. Scientists have found that tomato plants make high-pitched squeals when stressed!

Finger citron

This unusual citrus fruit looks like it has fingers! It has a lemony aroma that people use to scent rooms. It is thought by some to bring good luck.

Chocolate pudding fruit

The flesh of these fruits from the Caribbean and Central America is a dark mush that really does look like chocolate pudding. It is best in smoothies, jams, and pastries.

Jackfruit

Jackfruit, from India, are massive—they are the world's largest fruit to grow on trees. Their flesh has a firm texture and is cooked as a tasty alternative to meat.

Mango

Big mango trees can produce several thousand of these large stone fruits. They are originally from India, and when ripe, their flesh is sweet and has a strong scent.

Pineapple leaves are
sharp and spiky.

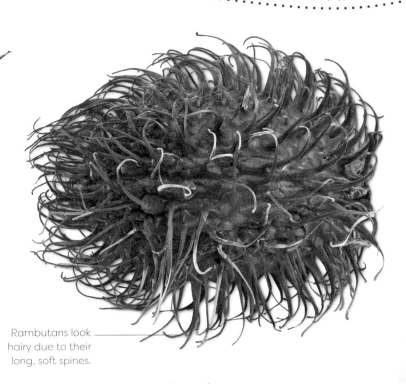

Rambutans look
hairy due to their
long, soft spines.

Rambutan

Originally from southeastern Asia,
rambutans are stone fruit the size of
hens' eggs. Orangutans and forest
birds love their white flesh, which
we cook into syrup or jam.

Pineapple

These spiky fruits come from Brazil.
Each one is actually made up of lots
of berries that have joined together.
Picked pineapples don't last long,
so their flesh is often canned.

Pomegranate

Peach

Seeds or stone?

Most fruits contain many seeds—pomegranates, for
example, have several hundred. Other fruits, such as
peaches, have a single, inedible, rock-hard seed, known
as a stone. They are called stone fruits, or drupes.

143

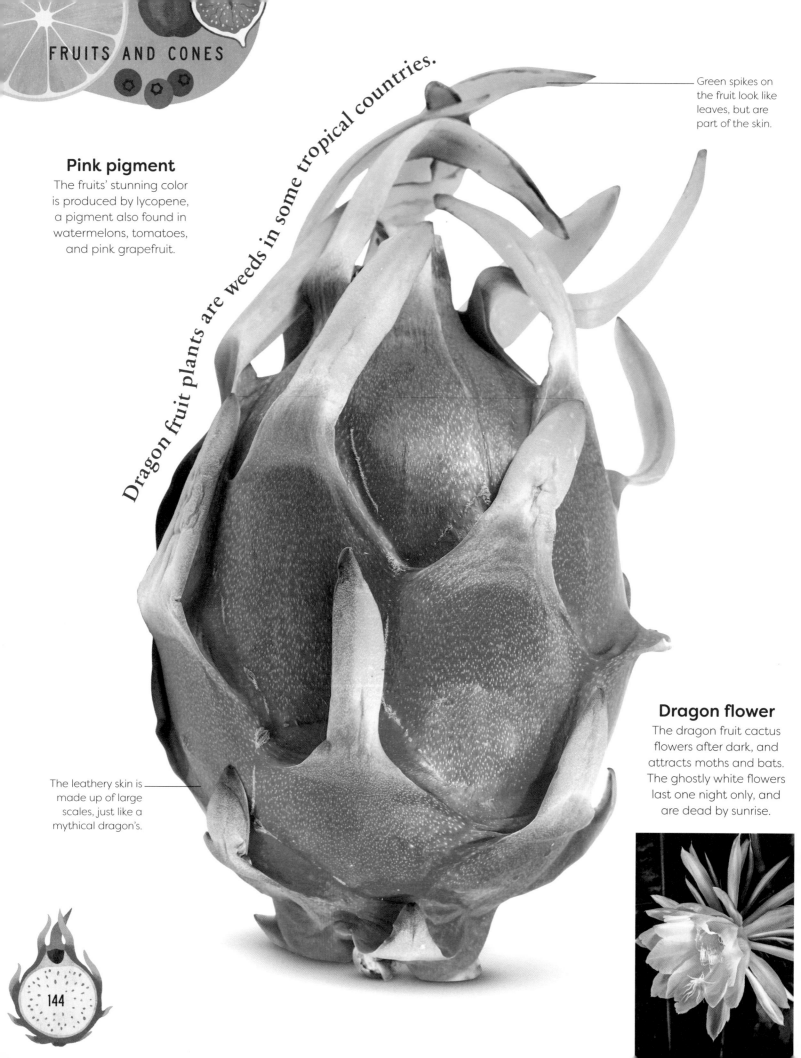

Pink pigment

The fruits' stunning color is produced by lycopene, a pigment also found in watermelons, tomatoes, and pink grapefruit.

Dragon fruit plants are weeds in some tropical countries.

Green spikes on the fruit look like leaves, but are part of the skin.

The leathery skin is made up of large scales, just like a mythical dragon's.

Dragon flower

The dragon fruit cactus flowers after dark, and attracts moths and bats. The ghostly white flowers last one night only, and are dead by sunrise.

144

Dragon fruit

The pink fruits of this tropical cactus look like they are covered in scaly dragon skin.

We don't often think of cacti as flowering plants, but they do blossom. They also produce fruits and seeds, like all flowering plants. Certain cacti fruits are edible and can be surprisingly sweet and refreshing. In deserts, they are an important source of freshwater for animals and humans alike. The dragon fruit cactus, though, lives in the tropical forests of Central America. Its spectacular fruits give the cactus its name, because their skin is colorful, tough, and scaly—like the dragons in myths. The other common name for these fruits is pitahayas, and they are also known as strawberry pears.

When you cut into dragon fruits, their flesh is just as attractive—it has black spots like a Dalmatian dog. Most people say the taste reminds them of kiwifruits, melons, and pears. The crunchy, black seeds are edible, too. Dragon fruit cacti must have a hot climate to bear fruit, but like many cacti, don't need much water. You can spot them in sunny gardens and courtyards all over the tropics, especially in southeastern Asia, where the fruit is a favorite.

White-fleshed dragon fruit
(*Selenicereus undatus*)
In its Central American home, the dragon fruit cactus often grows high up on trees. Its long stems trail from the branches.

White-fleshed dragon fruit

Yellow dragon fruit

Red-fleshed dragon fruit

Three of a kind
Most of the dragon fruits we see in shops and food markets have pink skin with white flesh. Two other types exist: one has yellow skin with white flesh, and the other has pink skin with red flesh.

Banana

The world's most popular fruit has many varieties, but one is eaten more than all the rest.

The curved shape of a banana is instantly recognizable. Except bananas don't always look like that. As baby fruit, they are straight! They become curved by growing away from the ground, toward the light. There are also hundreds of different varieties of bananas, not all of which develop a bend. Some are fat, thin, or very short, while their skin may be red or green. Certain varieties have tart flesh suitable only for cooking, but one sweet type is the global favorite. This is called the Cavendish. More than 100 million tons of Cavendish bananas are harvested each year.

The Cavendish banana has no seeds because we bred it that way to make it easier to eat. It is grown by cutting the underground stem into short sections, which sprout when planted in the soil. As a result, most of the banana plants grown on farms are identical copies, with exactly the same genes. This means they all produce the same delicious bananas. However, if a serious disease comes along that they are not immune to, it might wipe them all out—in fact, scientists are currently trying to fight a fungus infecting many Cavendish bananas.

Banana
(*Musa acuminata*)
There are many types of wild banana in eastern Africa and southern Asia. This variety is the ancestor of the popular Cavendish banana, which is grown in many tropical countries.

How bananas grow
Banana flowers are small tubes which hang from the plant in rows. They develop into bunches of fruit, known as hands, that start out green and pointing down toward the ground. The bananas take three to six months to mature into full-size yellow fruit, turning up toward the Sun as they ripen.

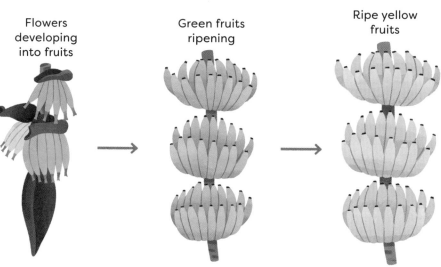

Flowers developing into fruits

Green fruits ripening

Ripe yellow fruits

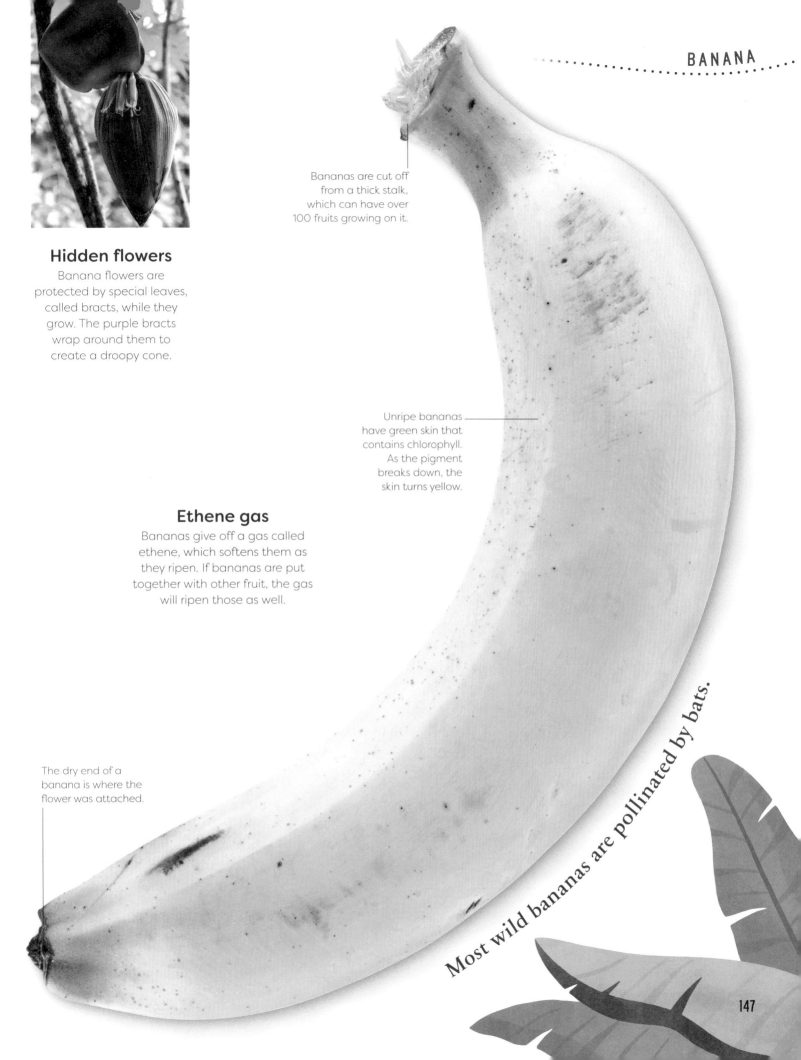

Hidden flowers

Banana flowers are protected by special leaves, called bracts, while they grow. The purple bracts wrap around them to create a droopy cone.

Bananas are cut off from a thick stalk, which can have over 100 fruits growing on it.

Ethene gas

Bananas give off a gas called ethene, which softens them as they ripen. If bananas are put together with other fruit, the gas will ripen those as well.

Unripe bananas have green skin that contains chlorophyll. As the pigment breaks down, the skin turns yellow.

The dry end of a banana is where the flower was attached.

Most wild bananas are pollinated by bats.

147

FRUITS AND CONES

Forest feast

Rain forests have thousands of different trees and vines, which bear fruit at different times. Fruit-eaters, such as this rhinoceros hornbill from southeastern Asia, can always find a fresh supply of ripe fruit somewhere in the forest. As they travel through the treetops, they scatter the seeds in their droppings.

Halloween pumpkins

Pumpkins grown for Halloween are a variety that is mostly hollow, with a flat bottom, which makes them much easier to carve and display.

The pumpkin's thick stem brings it nutrients from the vine.

Carved pumpkins are known as jack-o'-lanterns.

Pumpkin
(Cucurbita pepo)

Pumpkins are grown on most continents. Originally, like most other squashes, they came from Central America and the western half of South America.

A pumpkin becomes orange when ripe, but is green to begin with.

Squash bees

Pumpkin flowers are pollinated by little bees called squash bees. The females often dig their nests close to the developing pumpkins.

Pumpkin skin is leathery and waterproof.

Pumpkin

These heavyweight fruits grow on creeping vines that trail near the ground.

Some of our best-loved vegetables are actually fruit. Pumpkins, for example, are in fact monster berries! They belong to a large family of fruits that also includes squashes, cucumbers, melons, and zucchini. Pumpkins are bigger than all their relatives, however. Some varieties, when cultivated with great care, can be truly enormous. The world's heaviest ever pumpkin was grown in Italy in 2021 and weighed 2,703 lb (1,226 kg) when harvested—more than a small car! Usually, edible pumpkins take three months to reach full size. Their sweet, orange flesh is nine-tenths water, but highly nutritious. In the US and Canada, pumpkin pie is served at a traditional Thanksgiving dinner.

Pumpkins are an important part of the fall festival of Halloween, for which millions of them are grown every year. People hollow the pumpkins out by scooping out the pulpy flesh and seeds, then cut faces or patterns into their thick skin. Lights are sometimes placed inside so that they glow in the dark. This custom can be traced back to Ireland, where people used to carve turnips or fat potatoes to frighten off evil spirits.

Female flower

Developing fruit

Male flower

Pumpkin vine

A pumpkin vine is long and curly, and creeps sideways over the soil. If it reaches a post or fence, its tendrils twist around it for extra support. The vine's flowers are male or female. It is part of the fertilized female flowers that swell into pumpkins.

Pumpkin

Sticky seeds

Mistletoe seeds are smeared in a super-sticky goo. This helps them cling onto tree branches while they develop roots.

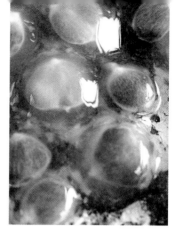

A black dot at one end of the berry shows where the flower was attached.

The berries are pea-size and have a hard, waxy skin. This one has been magnified many times.

Bunches of mistletoe decorate many homes at Christmas.

Toxic to some

Mistletoe berries are poisonous to humans, dogs, cats, and horses. Some birds, however, are able to eat them.

Mistletoe

Mistletoe takes root on branches and steals extra supplies from the tree to survive.

All kinds of folk stories have been told about mistletoe. This plant has always fascinated people because its leaves stay green throughout the year, even after the fall, when the trees it lives on drop their own leaves. In winter, green balls of mistletoe look wonderfully lush in the bare treetops. They may remind you of the nests of birds or squirrels. Our ancestors believed that mistletoe had magical powers, but there is a simpler explanation—it is a thief. Although it makes some food by photosynthesis, this is not enough for it to live on. Instead, using its roots, it invades its host tree to steal more nutrients, as well as water. Plants that live this way are called hemiparasites, which means "half-parasites."

You might be wondering how mistletoe gets into trees in the first place. It needs a helping hand from birds. Mistle thrushes and European blackbirds love its white berries but can't digest the seeds, which pass out in their droppings. The gooey seeds stick to branches like glue, and this is how the mistletoe moves from tree to tree.

Mistletoe
(Viscum album)
Mistletoe grows in balls in the branches of trees. There are over 1,000 types, with many found in tropical forests. This species lives in northern Africa, Asia, and Europe.

Sticking

Scattering

Moving around

Mistle thrushes feed on mistletoe berries, spreading the seeds in their poo. The seeds stick to the branches of their new host tree and send out a root that worms its way under the host tree's bark. The baby mistletoe plants then sprout leaves, and when grown, produce small flowers that turn into white berries.

Sprouting

Flowering

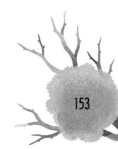

153

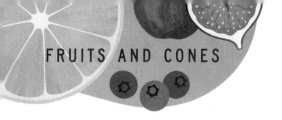
Lodgepole pine

Lodgepole pines produce thousands of beautiful cones that weigh down their branches.

Every woody cone made by a conifer tree is a natural treasure. Cones like these are always female. Conifers put their seeds in these armored containers to protect them from hungry herbivores. While the seeds ripen, the cone's tough scales, which originally developed from leaves, stay clamped shut. How, though, do the trees release their imprisoned seeds when they are ripe? The cones may open on their own during warm, dry weather to let the seeds spill out, and there are seed-eating mammals and birds that can crack them. Lodgepole pines use both these methods, but also have a third way. Sometimes, they bear cones that are sealed with a sticky liquid called resin. Only the intense heat of a forest fire will melt the resin to open the cones.

The trunks of lodgepole pines grow as tall and straight as pillars, making them valuable for lumber. They were traditionally used as the central poles in conical tents, called tepees, by certain Indigenous People of North America, including the Lakota people. This is how the trees got their name.

Lodgepole pine
(Pinus contorta)
Lodgepole pines form great forests in western North America, often by the coast and on the slopes of the Rocky Mountains.

Inside a cone
A female cone takes two years to mature. By this time, it is hard and woodlike, built from lots of tough scales. On every scale are two tiny seeds that are released when the cone opens.

Cone

Scale

Seeds

The woody cones of lodgepole pines hang under their branches.

The scales contain cellulose, the tough material also found in wood.

Spiral pattern
The scales are packed together around the outside of the cone in a series of spirals.

Prickles on the scales make the cone feel bristly.

The seeds are hidden near the center of the cone.

Runny resin
If a pine tree is damaged, it produces a thick, gluey substance called resin to seal any cuts. This drips down the tree's bark.

155

Male   Female

Male and female

Male cones, also called pollen cones, are small, soft, and loaded with pollen. Female cones have woody scales and are much larger. They are often called seed cones, because when pollinated, they slowly swell with seeds.

The woody cone may grow as big as a large pineapple.

Coulter pine

The female cones of this pine from California are the heaviest of any conifer. They can weigh more than a pet cat, so people working near the trees wear hard hats in case any fall off!

Kauri

This New Zealand tree's name is pronounced "koh-ree." The scales on its rounded female cones make beautiful spirals. Today, the kauri lives only in a few forests and is under threat from disease.

After three years, the cone collapses to scatter its seeds.

Cones

There are no flowers on conifer trees—they reproduce with cones instead. Cones can be male or female. Some species of conifers have both on the same tree, usually on different branches or at different times. In other species, trees are male or female, so only ever have one type of cone.

Lebanon cedar

The Lebanon cedar is origianlly from western Asia and the eastern Mediterranean. At first, its female cones are green. After pollination, they turn gray and woody and fatten into oval barrels.

Blue spruce

The sausage-shaped female cones of the blue spruce can be 4 in (10 cm) long. This North American tree has green-blue leaves, which give it its name.

Juniper

Unlike most conifers, juniper has female cones that are small and fleshy. These strongly scented cones look more like purple berries, and when ripe they are often called juniper berries.

Bristlecone pine

This rare pine grows on cold mountaintops, so its female cones are dark to help them warm up in the sun. It lives an incredibly long time—one tree known as Methuselah is over 4,850 years old.

Mediterranean cypress

Cypress trees produce round female cones that are about the same size as small marbles. The cones split to spread the seeds inside, but can also be opened by the heat of wildfires.

Douglas fir

The female cones of this North American tree are covered in prickles that stick out above the scales. The seeds inside are a favorite food of squirrels and other forest mammals.

Pollen cloud

Wind carries away the pollen stored in the male cones of pine and fir trees. It drifts through the forest in yellow clouds, which may be blown several thousand feet into the air. Most pollen ends up covering the ground like dust and is wasted, but by chance, a few grains land on female cones and pollinate them.

CHAPTER 6

Seeds and nuts

Seeds package up all the materials and instructions a new plant needs to grow. They can be smaller than a grain of sand or bigger than a basketball, and many are tough enough to survive years before sprouting. A selection of tree seeds were even taken into space, then planted safely on their return! Some fruits with hard outer casings look very like seeds, but with an extra protective coat—we call these nuts.

Brown bread

Brown bread, also known as "wholegrain bread," is made from flour that includes the seed coat from the wheat grains. This is removed to make white bread.

A million grains of wheat make 44 lb (20 kg) of white flour.

A tuft of hair at the top of the seed is known as a "brush."

The grain of wheat has a hard, brown coat, called bran.

Ancient grain

The ancient Egyptians farmed a type of wild wheat called einkorn, using water from the Nile River. An ear of einkorn is half the size of modern wheat.

Modern wheat grains are oval and up to 0.2 in (5 mm) long.

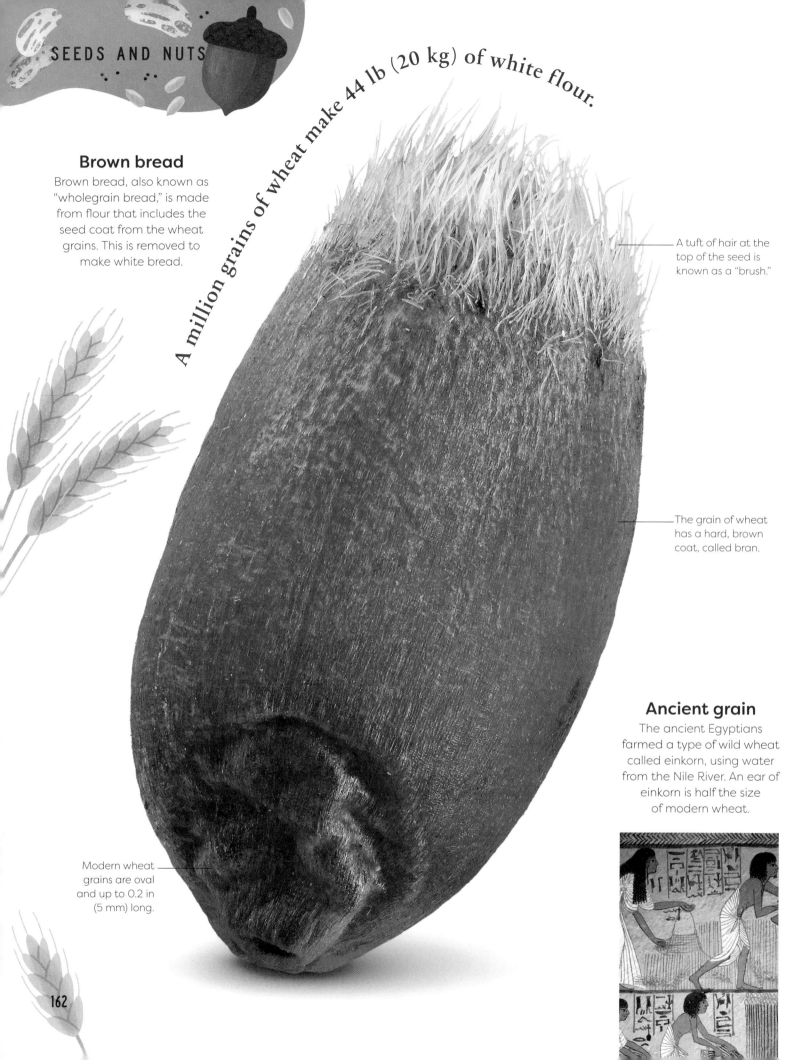

162

Wheat

Wheat has been grown for thousands of years, and is one of the most important crops the world has ever seen.

Some grasses have seeds we can turn into food. They are called cereal plants, and their seeds are known as grains. Wheat was the first cereal grown by humans, more than 10,000 years ago in the areas that are now Egypt, Iraq, and Turkey. Before then, many people moved from place to place to hunt animals and find wild plant food. Growing wheat allowed them to settle down and create some of the first farms and villages. These ancient farmers chose types of wheat that held onto the ripe grains at the head of the stalk, also known as an "ear." These varieties were easier to harvest than those that dropped all their grains on the ground.

Wheat grains are full of carbohydrates so they give us lots of energy, but they can't be eaten raw. They have to be turned into flour, which is baked or cooked. Today, wheat is used to produce all sorts of foods—from bread, noodles, and pasta to breakfast cereals, cakes, and sauces. Wheat is now often grown in huge fields that stretch as far as the eye can see. It is a thirsty crop so it needs massive amounts of water.

Common wheat
(Triticum aestivum)
Wheat is grown on every continent except Antarctica. The biggest producers are China, India, Russia, and the US.

Seed cases removed

Ears of wheat harvested

Grains crushed

Making flour

Ears of wheat are harvested with part of the stalk attached. They are beaten, or threshed, to remove the stalks. Air is then blown over them to remove the seed cases, known as chaff, leaving just the grains behind. The grains are finally crushed between steel rollers or heavy stones to produce the powder we call flour.

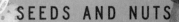

Tasty seeds

Edible seeds and nuts have always been important human foods. We eat them raw, or turn them into oil, spreads, or flavorings. Some seeds are major crops, including lentils, chickpeas, soy beans, and peanuts, which all belong to the pea family, and rice from the grass family.

Pistachio

We call these nuts, although they are actually seeds of the pistachio tree. The hard shells split to reveal the seeds, which are pale green with a purple seed coat.

Sunflower

The head of a sunflower is packed with 1,000–2,000 seeds, which are high in fat and protein. They are crushed to make cooking oil or consumed as a healthy snack.

Chickpea

Chickpeas are from southern Europe originally, but people cook with them all over the world. They are in fact lumpy seeds, and the pods they grow in are the fruits.

Lentil

Like the rest of the pea family, lentils develop in fleshy pods. Lentils were probably the first crop humans grew, as long as 13,000 years ago. They are cooked before being eaten.

Kola

Kola nuts, which are really large seeds, are made by a tree from western Africa. They contain twice as much caffeine as coffee! In the past, kola nuts were added to cola drinks.

Rice

Rice is the edible seeds of several grasses. The plants are grown in wet fields called paddies, mainly in Asia. The papery casing is removed to get to the seed, which is boiled or steamed.

Peanut

Peanuts are not nuts at all! They are unusual seeds, which form inside hard, wrinkly shells that grow under the soil. For this reason, they are also called groundnuts. Some people are very allergic to peanuts.

Each peanut shell usually contains one or two seeds.

Soy bean pods are covered in hair.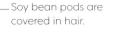

Soy

These seeds are half protein, so they are a useful alternative to meat, although they must be cooked to be safe to eat. Soy beans are often turned into other foods, such as tofu, but may also be used as feed for farm animals.

Seedlings and light

Once a seed has sprouted, it needs lots of sunlight to grow. Growing plants often bend toward the light, and a simple experiment, first carried out by the scientist Charles Darwin in the 1870s, shows that it is the tips of shoots that detect light. He covered the end of a shoot, so it was in the dark, and showed the plant grew straight up instead.

165

Corn

Corn is a global mega-crop that has changed enormously since farmers first grew it.

Popcorn, sweetcorn, and many other delicious foods come from corn. This plant, also known as maize, is a type of grass that grows rapidly to 10 ft (3 m) tall. At intervals along each stalk are cobs—sausage-shaped bundles of seeds wrapped in a green jacket and topped with a tassel. We call the seeds kernels, and they are why corn is such an important crop. Varieties of corn with sugar-rich kernels are harvested for people to eat, while others are grown as feed for cattle, or processed to make a liquid fuel called ethanol. The ethanol is often blended with gasoline and diesel to run vehicles!

The earliest corn farmers lived in southern Mexico around 9,000 years ago. They grew a wild corn, which was short and bushy, with much smaller cobs that held fewer kernels. Over several thousand years, tastier, larger cobs were produced. Corn was a very important food for the Aztec empire. The Aztecs had at least three gods associated with it, including Cinteotl, god of dried cobs of corn.

Corn kernel

Corn kernels used to have a tough case. This feature was removed by breeding, and makes the corn easier to harvest.

Some types of corn have bright, jewel-like kernels.

Teosinte

Modern corn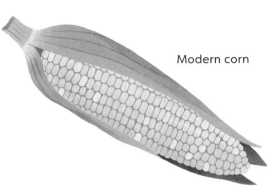

Changing corn

The ancestors of corn, called teosintes,
had small cobs with a few hard kernels.
Farmers selected plants with the best cobs
and the next year grew only their kernels.
Over many generations, the cobs became
larger, with softer, juicier kernels.

Corn

(Zea mays)

Corn belongs to a group of
grasses with edible seeds,
called cereals. Its wild
relatives lived in Mexico's
mountains.

The kernels are pea-size
and sit in neat rows that
cover the whole of the cob.

Underneath the
seeds is a hard
core to which they
are attached.

Colorful cob

Modern corn has golden kernels,
but in older varieties they may be
red, bluish-gray, green, or black.
Some gardeners still grow these
types because they are so pretty.

167

Coffee

The seeds of the coffee tree, called beans, make one of the world's favorite hot drinks.

People have been enjoying coffee for over 1,000 years. We are not sure who brewed the first cup, but according to an Ethiopian legend, the drink was discovered by chance. In this tale, a shepherd called Kaldi was looking after some goats in the mountains. One day, the goats became energetic and could not sleep, and Kaldi realized it was because they had eaten the seeds of coffee trees! He tried some, and found they had the same powerful effect on him. Coffee beans are contained in small red berries, which are also known as coffee cherries. Usually each cherry contains two beans with their flat sides pressed together. They are full of a strong chemical called caffeine—this is what makes coffee drinkers feel more awake and alert.

Coffee was first harvested in Ethiopia, but traders took the beans all over the Middle East and the Mediterranean, and eventually, coffee drinking spread throughout the world. Coffee trees are now widely grown in Africa, southern Asia, and Central and South America. The coffee beans were once sold in 132 lb (60 kg) sacks, but so much coffee is now produced, growers sell it in 1 ton (1 tonne) bags!

Coffee
(*Coffea arabica*)
Africa has many types of coffee tree, but this is the one people cultivated first and still grow most of. Its mountain home is in Ethiopia.

Coffee cherries

Raw beans inside cherry

Roasted beans

Inside a coffee cherry
Ripe coffee cherries are bright red. Inside each one is a pair of pale-colored beans. Before the beans are ready to use, they must be roasted, which turns them dark brown and brings out their flavor. The roasted beans are ground to a powder and added to hot water to make coffee drinks.

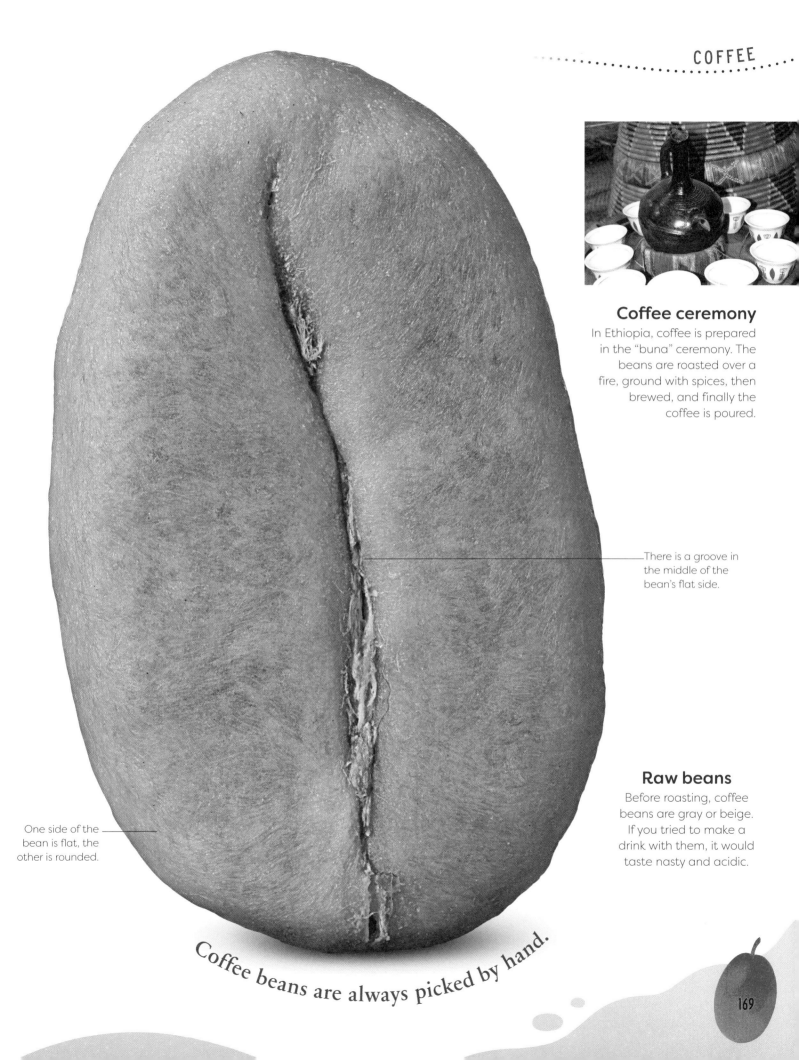

Coffee ceremony

In Ethiopia, coffee is prepared in the "buna" ceremony. The beans are roasted over a fire, ground with spices, then brewed, and finally the coffee is poured.

There is a groove in the middle of the bean's flat side.

Raw beans

Before roasting, coffee beans are gray or beige. If you tried to make a drink with them, it would taste nasty and acidic.

One side of the bean is flat, the other is rounded.

Coffee beans are always picked by hand.

Dandelion

Every dandelion seed has its own mini parachute to carry it away when it is ready.

Dandelions are often called weeds. What we mean is they like to grow where we don't want them. It is unkind to see dandelions as a nuisance, though. They are incredibly tough plants that deserve our respect. They flourish just about anywhere—even in patches of dirt by the roadside, on top of a wall, or in a crack in the pavement. How do they turn up in all those places? Dandelion seeds can fly! Every seed has a tuft of fine hairs that serves as a parachute. The seeds are loosely attached to the plant and weigh next to nothing, so the faintest breath of wind sends them on their way. Most move under 33 ft (10 m), but a few fly much farther, which is how dandelions reach new places.

Dandelion flower heads are made up of many small flowers, known as florets. There is one golden petal for each floret. The flower heads are rich in nectar and pollen, which feeds a wide variety of insects. Dandelions are actually better for pollinators than many other flowers we don't call weeds!

Common dandelion
(*Taraxacum officinale*)
Dandelions can be seen across Asia and Europe, their original home. They have now spread to many other parts of the world.

Spinning air
When a dandelion seed takes off, zones of spinning air form above it. These are created by the hairs of the parachute. The spinning air has a lower pressure and slows the seed as it falls, so that it drifts further before touching down.

Each dandelion produces around 100 flying seeds.

The tuft of wispy hairs is called a pappus.

Dandelion clocks

Once they have been pollinated, dandelion flower heads turn into silvery globes, known as clocks. They are made from masses of feathery seeds. The clocks are fragile and fall apart easily.

Secret signals

Dandelions have ultraviolet patterns, called nectar guides, that show insects where their pollen and nectar is. The markings are invisible to us because we can't see ultraviolet light.

Inside the brown case at the base of the parachute stem is a single tiny seed.

171

Desert in bloom

When rain falls in a desert, seeds waiting in the
sandy earth can sprout at last. Soon the entire area
explodes with plant life, as here in the Sonoran
Desert, which is in northern Mexico and southwest
US. Within a few weeks, the flowers produce seeds,
then wilt in the heat.

Jelly seeds

Cuipo seeds contain food for the new seedlings, as well as a special jelly that helps them soak up water from the soil.

The seed's stalk snaps in the wind to release it from the branch.

Nest site

Harpy eagles often build their nest in cuipo trees. They place the massive structure where a branch joins the trunk.

There are five large, paper-thin wings on each cuipo seed.

The seeds of cuipo trees are up to 5 in (12 cm) wide.

Cuipo tree

These rain forest trees have huge seeds that flutter as they fall to the ground far below.

Earth's tropical rain forests may have over 50,000 different types of trees. Many are hard to tell apart, but you won't miss cuipo trees, pronounced "kwee-poh." They soar above the trees around them. All of the cuipo trees in an area flower at once, as if they have received a secret signal. Their red blossoms can be seen for miles and is soon swarming with hawkmoths and hummingbirds. When these pollinators have done their job, the trees produce enormous seeds. The seeds have rounded wings that catch the wind, and swing to and fro on the ends of branches like brown paper lanterns. They hang there for a month while they ripen, then flutter to the forest floor, spinning as they go.

A cuipo tree's mighty trunk has no branches lower down and is much wider at the bottom. If you knocked on the smooth, gray bark, it might ring out like a gong! This is because the wood inside is very light, with less of the reinforcing woody material lignin than in other rain forest trees.

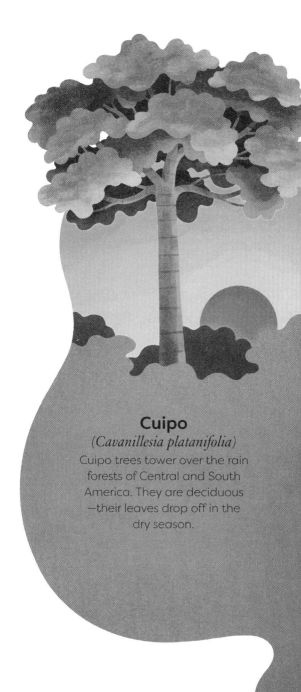

Cuipo
(*Cavanillesia platanifolia*)
Cuipo trees tower over the rain forests of Central and South America. They are deciduous —their leaves drop off in the dry season.

Carried on the wind

Most rain forest trees use animals to spread their seeds, but cuipo trees grow high above the rain forest canopy where the wind can easily reach them. They produce some of the largest winged seeds in the world, which are carried far away from their parent as they fall.

Acorn gall

Sometimes, a type of tiny wasp injects acorns with eggs and chemicals that make the nuts grow lumpy bits, known as galls. The wasp larvae develop inside the galls and feed on the acorn.

Acorns are apple-green at first, and turn brown as they ripen.

Each acorn sits in a holder, called a cupule, like an egg in an eggcup.

Acorn larder

North America's acorn woodpecker stores thousands of acorns in holes drilled into dead tree trunks. Each nut gets its own hollow.

Common oak

(*Quercus robur*)

This deciduous tree lives in most of Europe, except the north and south. Its acorns and wavy-edged leaves help to tell it apart from other trees.

A long stalk ends in
two or three acorns.

Oak

Forest animals collect large
numbers of oak tree nuts, called
acorns, to eat later.

Fall is a time of plenty for forest wildlife. This is when many
of the trees in cooler parts of the world produce their fruits. Some
are papery or juicy, but those of the oak tree, known as acorns, are
different. They have a tough shell around a single seed. Hardened
fruits like these are called nuts. Acorns make a nutritious meal for
lots of animals. Deer, wild pigs, and bears tuck in immediately, but
squirrels, mice, and colorful crows called jays are patient. They prefer
to carry the acorns away to bury throughout the forest. The hard
shells keep the seeds inside in perfect condition. During the
winter, when other food is hard to find, the clever animals
unearth their buried treasure and enjoy a feast!
Meanwhile, any acorns they forget about may
grow into oak seedlings.

Oak trees are long-lived and don't make acorns
until they are at least 40 years old. Some years,
they produce far more acorns than normal—
but why? The bumper crop fills the forest
with so many acorns that even more of them
will go uneaten and become new oak trees.

Storing acorns

The Eurasian jay gathers up to 5,000 ripe
acorns in the fall and stores them in many
different places. It relies on a kind of mind
map to remember where its hiding places
are, but always misses some acorns, which
sprout the following spring.

Eurasian jay

177

Field maple

Maple trees pack their seeds inside dry fruits that have wings to make them travel farther. The wings whirl in the air like the rotors of a helicopter. Winged fruit are called samaras.

At the base of each wing is a single seed.

Seeds for animals

Some plants rely on animals to spread their seeds in droppings after their fruits are eaten. Blackberry seeds are spread by birds, traveler's palm seeds by lemurs, and tucuma palm seeds by river fish. The seeds of violets attract ants that carry them away.

Blackberry fruit

Traveler's palm seeds

Tucuma palm fruit

Violet seed

Poppy seeds are just 0.04 in (1 mm) wide, and can grow after years in the soil.

Common poppy

The seedpod of this European wildflower dries into a papery box. When the wind gives it a shake, hundreds of tiny seeds are flung out of holes at the top.

Spreading seeds

Every plant that makes seeds must be able to scatter them so they don't fall straight to the ground. Otherwise, the new plants would compete for water, nutrients, and light with their parent. It's better to spread seeds far and wide, and plants have many ways of doing this.

Frémont's cottonwood

After pollination, the female flowers of cottonwood trees ripen into fluffy, white seedheads. On windy days, the fluff drifts through the air like a summer snowstorm.

Sea heart

Sea hearts, also called sea beans, are seeds from a tropical tree of the same name. They drop into rivers and are carried out to sea, to wash up on a faraway shore.

Tickseed

This flower develops into a prickly ball of hooked seeds. They stick to the fur of mammals—and our clothes! Once stuck, they hitch a lift and fall off somewhere else.

Brazil nut

This rain forest tree has woody fruits the size of cricket balls. Agoutis, which are like guinea pigs, crack them to eat their seeds. Any uneaten seeds may grow into new trees.

Sweet chestnut

These trees produce hard, shiny fruits, called chestnuts, found inside spiky, green cases. Squirrels and wild boars love chestnuts, and as they feed, help to spread the seeds inside.

Banksia

The winged seeds of Australia's banksia trees are made in tough containers, similar to pine cones. The cases stay shut until the intense heat of a wildfire splits them open.

The squirting cucumber fires seeds up to 20 ft (6 m) away.

Sudden sound

The seedpods of the sandbox, a tree found in the Amazon rain forest, explode violently with a loud bang!

Each seed inside a squirting cucumber fruit is hard and shiny.

Toxic cucumbers

Don't be fooled by this plant's name. It is distantly related to the cucumbers we eat but its fruits are poisonous.

Once the seed is on the ground, it sends out its first root from this end.

Squirting cucumber

When ripe, the fruits of the squirting cucumber fire their seeds long distances.

A few plants explode! This is not an accident—it can be an excellent technique for spreading seeds. The squirting cucumber is one of the plants that does this. In summer, it produces many small, green fruits, about the size of two pencil sharpeners placed end to end. They look a bit like miniature gherkins, but ripen in a different way. As each one grows, it fills with slimy juice, so the pressure inside its skin builds up. Eventually, the pressure is just too great and the fruit suddenly blasts off like a rocket ship! It breaks off the plant and surges forward, propelled by a jet of slime that shoots out of one end. In that slime are the plant's seeds, which are scattered as the fruit deflates like a balloon.

Some plants use another method to create their explosions. Their fruits do not fill with water—instead, they dry out. Gorse bushes are a good example. They have podlike fruits that lose water in warm weather and become fragile. Suddenly, the gorse pods split and fire seeds in every direction.

Squirting cucumber
(Ecballium elaterium)
This little plant is found in the Mediterranean. It likes dry, stony places with lots of sun.

Explosive seeds
The squirting cucumber has yellow flowers, and once bees have pollinated the female blooms, they develop into long, round fruits. The fruits swell with slimy juice until they are ready to burst, then pop off their stems. The force of the slime spraying in one direction powers the fruits the other way.

Coco de mer

Islands in the Indian Ocean have huge palm trees with the largest and heaviest seeds on Earth.

Species on islands sometimes turn into giants. As they adapt to island life over long stretches of time, they become larger than their cousins on the mainland. Giant tortoises now wander across the Galápagos Islands, there are giant hissing cockroaches on Madagascar, and islands in Indonesia are home to Komodo dragons, the planet's largest lizards. Like these creatures, coco de mer palm trees are enormous. Some stand as tall as an eight-story building, and they have immense flowers, fruits, and seeds. However, growing this big takes time. The monstrous fruits, which usually contain a single seed, spend over five years ripening. Each seed is up to 3 ft (1 m) around the middle and is probably too heavy for you to lift!

The first European sailors to see the seeds decided they must come from strange underwater trees on the seabed. They called the seeds coco de mer, which is French for "sea coconut." Today, only a few thousand of these wonderful palm trees are left. People now plant the seeds and guard the seedlings to save the species from extinction.

Coco de mer
(Lodoicea maldivica)
Coco de mer palms live on just two remote islands that form part of the Seychelles, an island nation in the Indian Ocean.

Rain collector
The coco de mer's leaves, which are the longest of any tree, fan out to catch rain. The water flows down a deep fold in each leaf toward the trunk, like the gutters on a house, then runs down the trunk to the soil, where the roots absorb it.

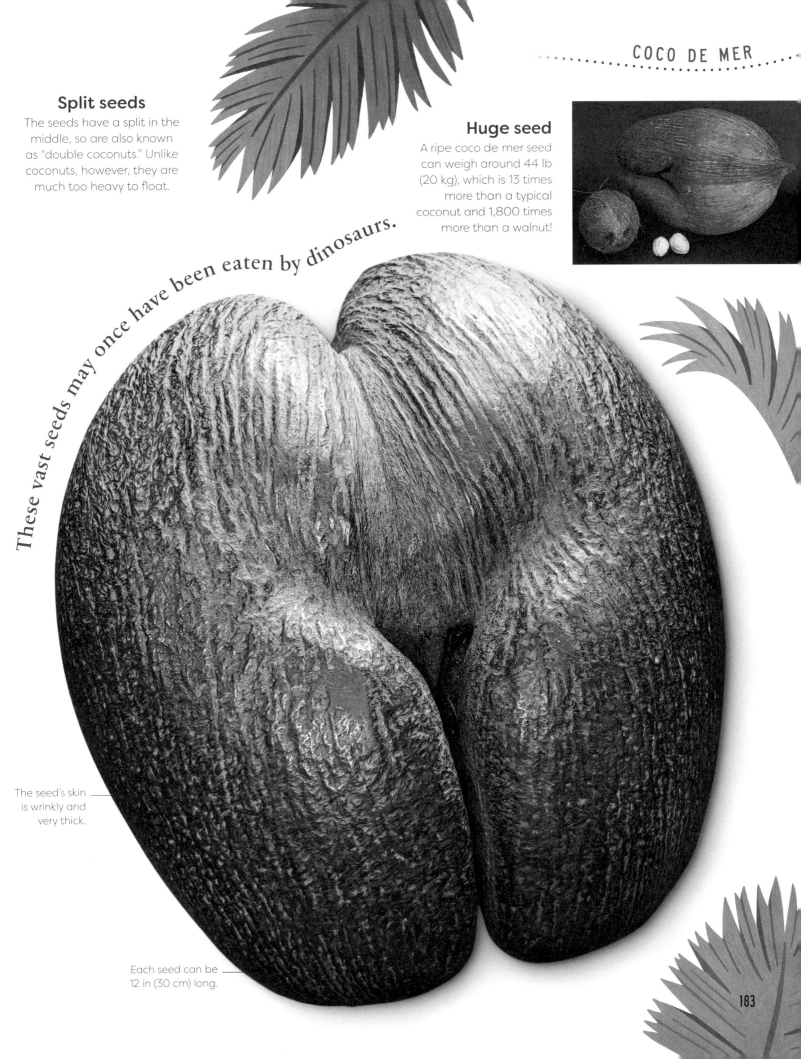

Split seeds

The seeds have a split in the middle, so are also known as "double coconuts." Unlike coconuts, however, they are much too heavy to float.

Huge seed

A ripe coco de mer seed can weigh around 44 lb (20 kg), which is 13 times more than a typical coconut and 1,800 times more than a walnut!

These vast seeds may once have been eaten by dinosaurs.

The seed's skin is wrinkly and very thick.

Each seed can be 12 in (30 cm) long.

183

National plants

Many countries have a national plant that is important to their people. It may even appear on their flag. For example, Canada's flag has a maple leaf.

Black walnut

This tree from the US does not like having neighbors. It releases chemicals that build up in the soil and weaken or kill other plants nearby.

Giant water lily

The vast leaves of this flowering plant float on lakes and pools in South America. They can be up to 8 ft (2.5 m) wide!

Plants of the world

We live on a planet full of plants. Most grow in a particular habitat or climate, and help shape the landscape and culture of these places. Others can cope with varied conditions and may be a familiar sight on several continents. Here are some of the most spectacular and unusual plants from across the globe.

Queen of the Andes

Named after the Andes mountains where it lives, this plant produces a mighty flower spike that grows up to 39 ft (12 m) high.

Heather
Heather covers huge open habitats, called moorlands, in northern Europe. In summer, it turns whole hillsides purple with its small flowers.

Date palm
People in western Asia have harvested the sweet fruits of this tree for thousands of years. Some varieties are eaten fresh, while others are dried first.

Sandwort
Sandwort is one of the highest living flowering plants. Its tiny blooms have been seen at over 20,000 ft (6,100 m) in the Himalayan mountain range.

Welwitschia
The Namib Desert is the only place on Earth where you can see this weird plant in the wild. It has two ribbonlike leaves and lives for up to 1,000 years.

Bat flower
This plant from southern Asia has black flowers, which are rare in nature. They are shaped like bat wings, with long threads like cat whiskers!

King protea
South Africa's national flower has huge blooms that look like crowns. They attract sugarbirds, which have curved bills to reach the nectar.

Australian Christmas tree
This tree is named for its orange flowers that appear in December. It is a parasite that steals food from plants near it.

Glossary

alga tiny organism, usually with only one cell, that mostly lives in water and makes food by photosynthesis. Seaweeds are large algae

anther top part of a flower's stamen that produces pollen

bark tough covering of tree trunks and branches that protects the wood underneath

berry type of fleshy fruit with one or many seeds, but no hard stone

blossoms flowers of some trees and bushes that usually cover the whole plant for a short period of time

bract type of leaf that protects the buds or flowers on some plants. Bracts can be colorful and look like petals

bud part of a plant that grows into a new shoot, leaf, or flower

bulb underground structure made by certain plants. It is formed from fleshy leaves and acts as a food store over winter or the dry season when the rest of the plant dies back

bulblet small bulb that forms on the side of a parent bulb. It separates to grow into a new plant

canopy continuous layer of branches and leaves formed from the treetops in a forest

carbohydrate type of substance made by living organisms, often as food. Sugars and starches are carbohydrates

catkin long cluster of male or female flowers produced by some trees, usually pollinated by the wind

cellulose tough material found in all plants. It is the main substance in the walls of plant cells

chlorophyll green substance in plant cells that absorbs the energy from sunlight and allows the cells to carry out photosynthesis

climate change long-term change in the temperature or weather of the Earth

clone organism that is an exact copy of another organism, with the same genes

cone structure made by some plants to protect their seeds or pollen. Female cones are woody and contain seeds, male cones are soft and contain pollen

coniferous description of trees with needlelike leaves and cones. Most conifers are evergreen

crop plant that is grown to be harvested for food, often in large fields. Rice and wheat are common crops

cultivation when a plant is grown by people. For example, in a farm, garden, or house

deciduous description of trees that lose all their leaves once a year, usually in a cold or dry season, and then regrow them. The leaves of deciduous trees often change color to yellow or red before falling off

drupe type of fleshy fruit that contains a single hard seed, or stone

endangered when a species is becoming rare and might go extinct

epiphyte plant that grows on another plant for support but does not take anything from it. Air plants are epiphytes

evergreen description of plants that have leaves all year round

extinct when all the individuals of a particular species have died out

fertilization when male plant cells from pollen join with a female plant cell in an ovary. This produces a baby plant, called an embryo, inside a seed

fertilizer substance used to make crops and other plants grow faster

filament long, thin stem of a flower's stamen with an anther at the top

frond long, leaflike structure in ferns

fruit structure that surrounds a plant's seeds. Fruits can be fleshy, such as a berry, or hard and dry, such as a nut

fungus living thing that usually grows in soil or on wood and gets its food by digesting the remains of plants and animals. Mushrooms, toadstools, and molds are parts of fungi

germination process in which a seed begins to sprout and grow into a new plant

heartwood very hard dead wood at the center of a tree trunk

host organism that another type of organism, called a parasite, takes nutrients from

hybrid offspring of parents from two different species. Hybrid plants are also called crosses

leaf structure that plants use to carry out photosynthesis and breathe. Leaves often have a flat upper surface, but can be needles, spines, or other shapes. They are usually green and filled with chlorophyll

lichen organism that is a partnership between an alga and fungus, which share a body

lignin extremely strong material found in some plant cells. Lignin and cellulose are the main materials in wood

lumber wood cut from a tree trunk for use in buildings or construction

nectar sweet liquid made by most flowers to attract and reward pollinators

nectar guide mark on a flower's petals that shows pollinators where the nectar lies

nut type of dry fruit with a hard shell that protects the seed inside. Acorns and chestnuts are nuts, but many other things we call "nuts," such as peanuts, are not true nuts

nutrient substance that helps a living thing grow. Minerals in the soil are important plant nutrients

ovary part of a plant that produces its female reproductive cells, usually found at the base of a flower. These cells merge with male cells during fertilization to form seeds, and the ovary becomes a fruit

parasite organism that benefits from another organism. For example, mistletoe is a plant parasite that steals nutrients and water from the host trees it lives on

petal part of a flower that is often colorful and scented to attract pollinators. Petals are a type of leaf

photosynthesis process by which plants make food. They do this by using the energy from sunlight to change carbon dioxide gas and water into sugars and oxygen

phytoplankton types of miniature plant that live in water, including single-celled green algae

pigment colorful substance. For example, the pigment chlorophyll makes leaves green

plant living thing that usually makes food from sunlight by photosynthesis. Most plants grow in soil and have leaves, stems, veins, and roots

poison toxic substance that will harm or kill an organism that eats or touches it

pollen tiny grains produced by male flowers or cones so a plant can reproduce

pollination when pollen is moved from the male anther of one flower to the female stigma of another flower of the same type

pollinator animal that transfers pollen from one flower to another and pollinates it. Pollinators include mammals, birds, and insects—for example, bees, wasps, and butterflies

resin thick, sticky liquid made by trees, especially conifers, to heal damaged bark or seal up ripening cones

rhizome type of underground stem that grows sideways to help some plants spread

root branching structure that anchors a plant and takes in water and nutrients, usually from the soil

runner type of stalk that spreads over the ground and produces buds that turn into new plants. Strawberry plants spread with runners

sap watery juice in plant cells

sapling young tree

seed structure produced by plants, usually inside a flower or cone, from which a new plant grows

seedhead structure that contains seeds, which develops from a flower in some plants

self-pollination when a plant pollinates its own flowers, without the need for a pollinator

sepal type of leaf at the base of a flower that protects its buds or petals

shoot growing stem of a plant, together with its leaves and flowers. When seeds sprout, they send out a shoot

sorus small structure on the underside of fern fronds that contains spore-making factories, called sporangia. Sori are often circular

species type of organism. Members of the same species can breed together and usually look similar

spore dustlike particle similar to a seed that mosses, ferns, and fungi use to spread

stamen male part of a flower that includes an anther, which produces pollen, and a filament

stem stalk that supports a plant and transports water and nutrients. Stems can be soft or woody

stigma female part of a flower that receives pollen

stomata microscopic holes in a leaf through which plants breathe. Most stomata are found on the underside of leaves and close up at night

strobilus lumpy or conelike structure that makes spores, which is found in some plants that lack flowers, such as horsetails

tendril thin stalk that twists and curls around objects for support

tropical description of the warm regions surrounding the Equator

trunk woody, bark-covered central stem of a tree

tuber type of underground stem or root that some plants use to store food

vascular description of plants that use networks of tubes to transport water and dissolved nutrients

vein tube that gives a leaf strength and holds it in shape, and that carries water, sugars, and other nutrients around the plant

virus type of life form that can cause disease by infecting plants, animals, or other living things

wildfire fire that starts naturally in a dry place or season. Climate change is making wildfires hotter and more frequent

Index

Author Ben Hoare
Illustrator Kaley McKean

Project Editor Olivia Stanford
Designer Sonny Flynn
Senior Art Editor Kanika Kalra
US Editor Jill Hamilton
US Senior Editor Shannon Beatty
Senior Production Editor Nikoleta Parasaki
Senior Production Controller Isabell Schart
Senior Picture Researcher Sakshi Saluja
Senior DTP Designer Neeraj Bhatia
Managing Editor Jonathan Melmoth
Managing Art Editor Diane Peyton Jones
Deputy Art Director Mabel Chan
Publishing Director Sarah Larter

Consultant Dr. Jonathan Mitchley

First American Edition, 2022
Published in the United States by DK Publishing
1745 Broadway, 20th Floor, New York, NY 10019

Text copyright © Ben Hoare 2022
Copyright © 2022 Dorling Kindersley Limited
DK, a Division of Penguin Random House LLC
23 24 25 26 10 9 8 7 6 5 4
008–329156–Oct/2022

A catalog record for this book
is available from the Library of Congress.
ISBN 978-0-7440-5983-0

DK books are available at special discounts when purchased
in bulk for sales promotions, premiums, fund-raising, or
educational use. For details, contact:
DK Publishing Special Markets,
1745 Broadway, 20th Floor, New York, NY 10019
SpecialSales@dk.com

Printed and bound in China

For the curious
www.dk.com

DK would like to thank: Gary Ombler for photography; Oxford Botanic Garden & Arboretum for kindly allowing us to photograph their plants; Ahmed Bilal for picture research; Simon Mumford for cartography; Caroline Hunt for proofreading; and Helen Peters for the index.